posh crosswords

(75) PUZZLES

The Puzzle Society™
puzzlesociety.com

D0785330

Andrews McMeel
Publishing, LLC

Kansas City

08 09 10 11 12 LEO 10 9 8 7 6 5 4 3 2 1

ISBN-13: 978-0-7407-7278-8
ISBN-10: 0-7407-7278-3

Cover design:
Mocca © 2003 The Alexander Henry Fabrics Collection

www.andrewsmcmeel.com
www.PuzzleSociety.com

ATTENTION: SCHOOLS AND BUSINESSES
Andrews McMeel books are available at quantity discounts with bulk purchase for educational, business, or sales promotional use. For information, please write to: Special Sales Department, Andrews McMeel Publishing, LLC, 4520 Main Street, Kansas City, Missouri 64111.

posh crosswords

75 PUZZLES

FILMING GEOMETRY

By Isaiah Burke

ACROSS

1 Stallone role
6 Sanction misdeeds
10 Remove holes
14 One way to set a clock
15 Shady route
16 Skin-cream ingredient, perhaps
17 1956 crime drama (with "The")
20 Hardly exciting
21 Former British prime minister Wilson
22 Protective shelter
25 Temperamental star
28 Source for a movie, often
29 On the fence
33 Had been
34 Ritchie Valens classic
35 Means to a diagnosis
37 1959 comedy with Anna Neagle (with "The")
43 Glance over
44 "The Pink Panther" director Edwards
46 Day-after-Christmas event
50 Social protocols
53 Arkin and Alda
55 Like contented bugs
56 Braying beast
57 Bean or noodle
59 Violist's clef, perhaps
62 1989 war film
68 Garner

69 Pride sound
70 It connects levels
71 To be, to Brutus
72 Superficially cultured
73 Land on the Sea of Japan

DOWN

1 Vied for office
2 "Eureka!"
3 Debussy's "La ___"
4 Shakespeare, for one
5 Olfactory property
6 Means of exoneration
7 Embargo
8 Chang's twin
9 It follows Georgia in higher education
10 Monkey Trial attorney
11 Recess or small room
12 Word with derby or coaster
13 Compass part
18 African ravine
19 Actor Holm
22 Pot top
23 Organic compound
24 U.S. poet Millay
26 Niacin, for one
27 Roman greetings
30 It's sometimes bitter
31 Low-lying islands
32 Title for an atty.
36 Toothpaste container
38 Truman's successor, popularly
39 Isn't off one's rocker?

40 Short elevation
41 Pro ___ (in proportion)
42 Barely makes do (with "out")
45 Feminine suffix
46 River formed by the Congaree and Wateree
47 Oahu greetings
48 Some brews
49 Wankel or diesel
51 Stone pit
52 Homely fruit?
54 Recruit's sentence ender, perhaps
58 Nick Charles' wife
60 To-do list item, perhaps
61 Having knowledge of
63 Neither fish ___ fowl
64 Create knotted lace
65 Predatory fish
66 Canard
67 Division of history

CHECK IT OUT
By Ruth Keller

ACROSS

1 Counterpart
5 Muscle contraction
10 Beginning of relief?
14 Allies' adversary
15 Type of black tea
16 Cap setting
17 Some checks
20 Gucci of fashion
21 Prefix for classical or Latin
22 Finish the course?
23 Opposite of deject
26 ___ Dawn Chong
28 Words with the chase
30 Some checks (with 49-Across)
33 Tourmaline, e.g.
34 Appease fully
35 Make a right
36 "Watermark" chanteuse
38 "Beauty and the Beast" character
40 Nursing a grudge
44 Vientiane native
46 Hebrides isle
48 Recess game
49 See 30-Across
54 Interior style
55 End of some Web addresses
56 Pains in the neck
57 Get behind, in a way
58 Gig implement
60 Dele undoer
62 Some checks
68 Jungian topics

69 Get ready for kickoff
70 Superior, for one
71 Adam's boy
72 Marching drum
73 Checked out with interest

DOWN

1 Make imperfect
2 Firefighter's tool
3 "Whether ___ nobler ..."
4 Executorial concern
5 Future fries
6 Make a long, grandiloquent speech
7 Bit of rap sheet shorthand
8 Elizabeth Barrett Browning work
9 Apportion
10 Take on moguls?
11 Coves
12 A frozen dessert
13 Memorable Moses portrayer
18 Baldwin, Guinness and others
19 Game often played with wooden balls
23 Good thing to have when competing
24 Legal claim
25 Type of ant
27 Artist's studio
29 Maui melody makers, briefly
31 Off-limits
32 Insurance promoter
37 Brand for Bowser

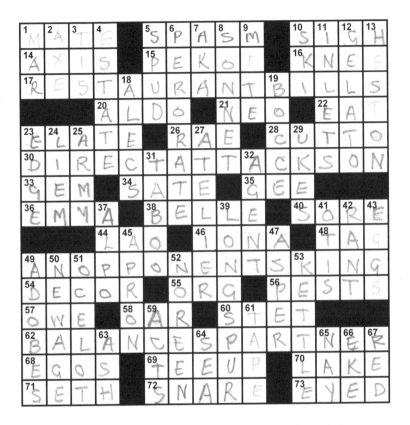

39 Bird with brownish plumage
41 Sheriff Taylor kept a cell for him
42 Spew fire and brimstone
43 Faberge handiworks
45 Kitchen cover-up
47 By order of
49 Sun-dried bricks
50 Section in a music store
51 Spotted wildcat

52 Corcoran of "Bachelor Father"
53 It lets off steam
59 It comes before Romans
61 Word with deck or measure
63 Silvery gray
64 Caribbean, e.g.
65 Vocal objection
66 Barely make (with "out")
67 Clearly embarrassed

WALK ON BY

By Donald L. Blocher

ACROSS
1 Ark landfall
7 Tarradiddle
10 Eye-opening problem?
14 Commit a card sin
15 You may walk on it
17 City near Bismarck
18 Prime minister before Gladstone
19 Homo sapiens, e.g.
21 Beverage in a jug, perhaps
22 Bit of buffoonery
24 Embargo
25 Operational lines?
28 Profound state of unconsciousness
30 Kind of roof
33 Whets the appetite
35 It equips you for a moving experience
36 Payment at some destinations
37 ___ fixe (obsession)
38 Place for a boxing match, perhaps
40 Take a shine to
41 Penitential period
42 Chocolatier's need
43 Plunderer
45 Half a figure-eight
46 Not as antiquated
48 Annuls
49 Greek dawn deity
50 Mothering sort
52 Moor

55 Most likely to elicit a pucker
59 Frigid edifice
63 Certain NFL pro
64 You may walk on it
65 Crazy Horse's people
66 Some Oriental beans
67 Prefix with Latin
68 Decorous

DOWN
1 Kind of race
2 Realize, as profits
3 Queenly name
4 You may walk on it
5 Versus
6 Creed component
7 Doctor of law degree (Abbr.)
8 Second sequel tag
9 Ems divided by two
10 Like a murdered dragon
11 Like a readied golf ball
12 December noun
13 Arabian prince
16 They may put on a whale of a show
20 Order to a dog
23 Broke a commandment
24 Predictably trite
25 Turn attachment
26 Hands over
27 Shouts with hands raised, sometimes
29 Date or age beginning
30 Part of the Antilles

31 Peeved
32 They may try you
34 Economizes
36 You may walk on it
39 Unpurified
44 Not young enough
46 "Not at all," vernacularly
47 Decay
49 Spirit of a culture
51 Plants used to make poi

52 Chart toppers
53 Sound for a spelunker
54 High-altitude habitation (Var.)
56 Dutch cheese
57 Peddle
58 Caterer's item
60 Footed vase
61 Take to court
62 Maniacal leader

SOLID AS A ROCK

By James E. Buell

ACROSS
1 Chords define them
5 Infield cover
9 Makes like a couch potato
14 The Motown Sound
15 Hodgepodge
16 Big man in Miami
17 Ecclesiastic title, in France
18 Street-closing festival, perhaps
20 Ersatz opening
22 Average guys
23 Crankcase contents
24 Scarlet letter, e.g.
26 Untidy place
28 Said of an active person
30 Ricky Martin's life
31 Quilters' gatherings
32 Road runner
34 Attention-getting joint
38 "The Big Band," for one
39 Slightly irritated
41 Praising poesy
42 Hayseed
44 College appointment
45 Sartre's "No ___"
46 Bravos of a sort
48 Some are stolen
50 First event in a series
53 Kyoto entertainer
54 Role for Mae
55 Exultant joy
57 Disgraces
60 Boy Scout's creation
63 McCay's "Little" one

64 Rise above
65 Dublin's country
66 Nursery fixture
67 Requisites
68 Legal title
69 They make a point on hobbits

DOWN
1 Chop-chop!
2 Rips off
3 A cut of tenderized beef
4 They follow trails
5 Kind of sled
6 The whole nine yards
7 Dry, Spanish red wine
8 Somewhat, musically
9 Askew
10 Collection of informative
   snippets
11 0000
12 Hit for "Weird Al"
13 With guile
19 French military hat
21 Sputter and stall
25 Piles of earth
27 "For Me and My ___"
28 Do as directed
29 Rex's detective
30 "Star Trek" trip
33 The third O of OOO
35 Brownie, e.g.
36 Comic strip canine
37 Throws water on, e.g.
39 Brisk tempos

40 Joined up

43 Millions of years

45 Upgrade

47 First name in courtroom fiction

49 Type of tray

50 "Maximus to Gloucester" poet Charles

51 Wound the pride of

52 Wash out with solvent

53 Lamp denizen

56 Achieved laboriously (with "out")

58 Middle Eastern royalty

59 Weeps convulsively

61 Include

62 Smeltery supply

PETTY BEGINNINGS
By Ruth Keller

ACROSS

1 32nd in a noted series
4 What a rolling stone will not be
9 Sails close to the wind
14 "... good witch ____ bad witch?"
15 Fumble around in the dark, e.g.
16 Like a feeble old woman
17 Twin-hulled boat
19 Twine material
20 Word from the pews
21 Acrobats' securities
22 Old alternative to regular
23 Goods carried by a large vehicle
25 Where to find many an ancestor
26 They have to face the music
30 Grammy category
33 Morocco's capital
36 Nursery supply
37 Roman god of love
38 Spew out
39 Travesty
40 Source of misery
41 Very urgent
42 Russian city founded in 1716
43 Roller coaster's island
44 Peculiar
45 Circuit device
47 Shropshire sounds
49 Reach one's goal, e.g.

53 Quarters in quads
55 Resting upon
58 Hence
59 Not suitable
60 Swimming stroke
62 Subway entrance, e.g.
63 Got it wrong
64 Seemingly forever
65 Copier additive
66 Ripened ovules
67 Wynken and Blynken's partner

DOWN

1 Type of point
2 Emotional series of events
3 Assessed
4 Famed movie studio
5 Agent of the Vietnam War?
6 Painful
7 Small fight
8 Itchings and hankerings
9 Light-producing devices
10 Merge
11 One angling for dinner?
12 Tear with a whip
13 Auction off
18 Bring to life
24 "The Confessions of ____ Turner"
25 Hefty volume
27 Doesn't just close
28 Some Rodins
29 Gets ready to break

31 First-class
32 Fair game
33 Overhaul
34 In the center of
35 Loon
37 Canceled a space mission
39 Competitors
43 Folding bed
45 Certain set of horizontal lines
46 Accessed (with "into")

48 More than enough
50 "Our Miss Brooks"
51 Inuit home
52 What may be in sight?
53 Do some housecleaning
54 Words with latch or catch
55 Some fruit drinks
56 Lacerated
57 Fairy-tale monster
61 They can get personal

ALL THE MAKINGS
By Alex Rich

ACROSS

1 Clumsy fellows
5 Town in Georgia or France
10 For men only
14 Quebec native
15 Kentucky Derby winner ___-Dale
16 Poi plant
17 It's in oranges
19 Big Apple stage award
20 Manipulative people
21 Nursery rhyme residence
22 Automobile pioneer Ransom
23 Secondhand deal
25 Make violently angry
27 Swiss hero
29 Actor Romero
32 Wingless parasites
35 State of agitation
39 Draft drink
40 "Sweet as apple cider" girl
41 Natural gas constituent
42 Grazing ground
43 Long time span
44 Wes of the NBA Hall of Fame
45 Milestone for baby
46 Armada
48 Word with jab or turn
50 It's known for its rings
54 Where I'll see you, tunefully
58 Without slack
60 Fuel from bogs
62 O founder
63 Prod

64 Refrigerator freshener
66 Nurture
67 County in Colorado or New Mexico
68 Oil-rich sultanate
69 Not any, colloquially
70 Egret or heron, e.g.
71 Anthroponym

DOWN

1 Transpire
2 Come to light
3 Throws a party for
4 Cut sharp notches into
5 Apple offering
6 "What a pity!"
7 Hiding place
8 Gibson garnish
9 2000 presidential candidate
10 Howard, Fine or Howard
11 It's at most meals
12 Like the Badlands
13 Proceeds
18 "Robinson Crusoe" locale
24 Oscar winner Burstyn
26 43,560 square feet
28 Back muscles, for short
30 To the sheltered side
31 Gather from the fields
32 Shakespearean "gladly"
33 Word with teen or matinee
34 Honey alternative
36 The T in "GWTW"
37 Where there may be a mess?

38 Called it off
41 Mongrel canine
45 Greg, to Carol Brady
47 Greasy spoon, e.g.
49 Type of edible legs
51 Certain violin stroke
52 "Giant" ranch
53 Like skinny-dippers

55 It often hangs around the kitchen
56 Sir's counterpart
57 Classic Western
58 Go sour
59 Carpeting calculation
61 Part of the landing gear
65 Here-there connection

DANCE FOR ME

By Alice Walker

ACROSS

1 Some mantel pieces
6 Holiday helper
9 "___ not amused"
14 Prefix for mural or venous
15 Opening for a maid?
16 Baseball Hall-of-Famer Monte
17 Trace, as of hope
18 What a kid may say
19 Broadway luminaries?
20 Dessert choice, perhaps
23 Pertaining to the eyes
24 Used a backhoe, e.g.
25 Liveliness
26 Cyberspace initials
29 Passover breads
34 Rainy day amusement, perhaps
37 Soup du jour, sometimes
40 ___ Lanka
41 Star observer
42 Author of inspirational stories for boys
45 Malmo locale
46 Where to find good schools?
47 "No ___" (sign in certain restaurants)
50 They assist MDs
52 Long, slender sword
55 Befuddle
60 Currency in 40-Across
61 Intention
62 Member of a Jamaican religion

63 Disburdened
64 Reggae relative
65 Highest stages
66 Dude, to a Brit
67 Certain layer
68 Timothy who took many trips

DOWN

1 Type of circus
2 Prepare to remove an ice skate
3 Increase, as the pace
4 Follow the leader
5 American or Western follower
6 Thompson of "Howards End"
7 Bissextile year
8 Charlatan
9 Anemometer
10 Part of a palindrome
11 Shakespeare's river
12 Pug's place
13 Running's three
21 Rugged cliff
22 Hauler's destination, sometimes
27 ___ buco
28 "___ Theme" ("Doctor Zhivago" tune)
30 Former Russian ruler
31 Sound asleep?
32 Cheer for a bullfighter
33 Rev.'s oration
34 Family name in "The Grapes of Wrath"

35 Help mediate a conflict
36 ___ E. Coyote
37 Expressions of understanding
38 This very moment
39 Intense outrage
43 Words with uncertain terms
44 Distinctive clothing
47 Foreboding atmosphere
48 Irish hunting dog, for one
49 Type of spoon

51 Kind of hit
53 Ear-related
54 Word with mat or kick
55 Twofold
56 ___ facto
57 Use a search engine
58 Human-powered vehicle
59 Arabian monarchy
60 Fighter at Vicksburg, briefly

POOR MAN, RICH MAN

By Isaiah Burke

ACROSS

1 Spread unchecked
5 Union nemeses
10 Scottish social unit
14 Seth's older brother
15 Surfer's enabler, perhaps
16 George Eliot's "Felix ___, the Radical"
17 Poor way to live
20 Classified words
21 "Runs like ___" (sales pitch for a used car)
22 Fall behind
23 Tire reinforcement
24 King beater, in pinochle
25 Contemptible fellow
28 Paradise lost
30 Petal-plucker's word
32 Land attachment?
34 Prognosticator's forte, maybe
37 They share the same atomic number
39 Lavish way to live
42 First Earl of Beaconsfield
43 Prospector's find
44 Nickel finish?
45 "Oh, what's the ___?"
47 Title role for Jodie Foster
51 Social register word
52 Veto
54 Take your pick
57 Classic prefix
58 "Beloved" author's first name
59 Commercial fuel

61 Poor way to live
65 Vicinity
66 Silly
67 "Miracle Mets" outfielder
68 Kind of trap
69 Daisylike bloom
70 G-men and T-men, e.g.

DOWN

1 Kind of ticket
2 Across the sea, perhaps
3 First name of three presidents
4 Trees in an O'Neill title
5 Kind of change
6 Some rabbits
7 Check the check
8 Electronic trial
9 Dealt a mighty blow
10 Kind of stick
11 Apt name for a restroom attendant?
12 Cockpit abbr.
13 Imprecise ordinal
18 Occur by chance
19 Chimera, for one
25 Major mafioso
26 Take down ___ or two (humble)
27 Front for Plaines
29 Part of UNCF
31 Erstwhile music players
33 Humorist Myron
35 Irish river
36 "The Conqueror Worm" poet

38 Utterance of discovery
39 It's often tanned
40 Soothsayer's words
41 Continual changes
42 Syndicate head
46 Epoch between Paleocene and Oligocene
48 What gears do
49 Pressured (with "on")
50 Setbacks

53 Vasco da Gama destination
55 Baffling problem
56 Beret kin
58 Type of stool
60 Table part, perhaps
61 ___-relief
62 Stage of history
63 Yearning
64 William Styron subject Turner

BAD WEATHER

By Harold Bentley

ACROSS

1 Street vernacular
6 Livorno currency, once
10 Certain construction beam
14 Black thrush
15 Teapot tempests?
16 Artist's inspiration
17 Alternate passage indicator, in a score
18 Where soldiers are made
20 Flabbergasted
22 Clothes line
23 ___ de la Cite
24 Weave go-with
25 Crackpot
28 "Look ___ ye leap"
29 Wax eloquent
31 Permeates moistly
33 Heady draft
34 Sneaky-laugh sound
36 Deck-planking wood
37 Concerns for ecologists
40 Aka Deseret
42 Hockey legend
43 A/C capacity measurement
44 Chinese-food order request, perhaps
46 Part of IV
48 "Shoo!" on the farm?
51 Socially emerging young woman
52 It may be heroic
54 One-time White House nickname

55 It contains genetic info
56 Blistering
60 Ignore the alarm
62 Erode
63 Cubbyhole
64 Type of exam
65 More than double
66 Defeats regularly, in slang
67 Italy's Villa d'___
68 Divided, as real estate

DOWN

1 Offer comfort to
2 More opulent
3 Presuppose
4 Nuremberg negative
5 Flower shop purchases, sometimes
6 Famous tar pits
7 Words that bond
8 Type of float
9 Member of the Jetson's family
10 Computer that came in many colors
11 Crummy joints?
12 Dangerous reptile
13 Solfege syllables
19 World Series winners of 1908 and not since
21 City in Oklahoma
26 "___ lazy river ..."
27 "For shame!"
30 McCullough's "The ___ Birds"
32 Words to Brutus

33 Massage reactions, perhaps
35 Burial site for Abraham and Sarah
37 Talk and talk and talk ...
38 Squanders little by little (with "away")
39 "The Girl From Ipanema" saxophonist
40 Berlin connection
41 Musician's tapper
45 Comic's collection

47 Almost a home run
48 How some potatoes are served (with "au")
49 Ready for a commitment?
50 Made some lace
53 Lover of Daphnis
57 Rankles
58 Shipshape
59 Casino game
60 Lennon's mate
61 Formal promise

TEMPER, TEMPER
By Marcus Candley

ACROSS
1 He went for baroque
5 Siamangs, e.g.
9 Spending spell
14 Ruffle feathers
15 Book in the Bible
16 Least favorite pet?
17 Swedish statesman Palme
18 Part of QED
19 Shakespearean forest
20 Snapped
23 "I'm outta here"
24 Senor Guevara
25 Letters on a dumbbell
28 It may be bitter
29 Classic toy
33 Young equine
34 New Zealand native
35 Bonaire neighbor
36 Became very angry
41 Kind of supervision
42 Postulation
43 Theater section
44 Corkscrew
46 One toward passage
49 Some B'way letters
50 Word with Rio or Mar
51 Best part of the cake, to some
53 Lost one's cool
58 Type of situation
60 Yucky stuff
61 Speller's phrase
62 Examinations of a type
63 Knife handle

64 Established custom
65 Rich cake
66 Thence
67 Is litigious

DOWN
1 Look around casually
2 Quinn in "Annie"
3 Made a replica
4 Stalwart
5 Floor measure
6 Knit partner
7 Citation ender, briefly
8 Comic's routine
9 Sudden outpouring
10 Persian fairy
11 Colorful Sioux chief?
12 Three-faced woman?
13 Poetic time of day
21 Volcanic rock
22 Just short
26 Hindi courtesy title
27 Duel prelude
30 Chat room chuckle
31 Capone's nemesis
32 Contemporary of 31-Down
33 Raised area on a neck
34 Form check box, perhaps
35 Aviator Earhart
36 Women, condescendingly
37 Redolence
38 Back-and-forth contest
39 Auction suffix
40 Certain literary collection

44 Create a dart
45 Sorry state
46 Greek toast "To your health"
47 It could stall
48 Star pitchers
50 Slow on the uptake
52 Animal stomachs

54 Jaunty rhythm
55 Life preserver?
56 Vegetarian staple
57 Makes a choice
58 "Like it" alternative
59 Gold, in Guatemala

SOFT SOAP
By Georgia Flavin

ACROSS
1 Puts on the clock
6 Deep-seated desire
10 Asian desert
14 One of Cain's sons
15 Kind of book or will
16 Parched
17 Soap opera
20 Prohibit, presidentially
21 Language spoken by Jesus
22 Poetic before
23 Face-to-face exam
24 Capital of Tibet
28 Gown features, often
30 High and low
32 French port city
35 ''___ been working on the railroad ...''
36 Soap opera
40 Missile defense initials
41 ''Sergeant ___ of the Yukon''
42 ''Guernica'' painter
45 Chronicles
49 Sprain site
50 It's offered in a hospital
52 It may elicit a call
53 Like an increase from two to twenty
56 Like some hair
57 Soap opera
61 Of all time
62 Has attachment
63 Ryan of ''The Beverly Hillbillies''
64 Caddie's bagful
65 Named names
66 Critical evaluations

DOWN
1 Billows
2 Certain newspaper ad
3 British bad guy
4 It may bounce off the wall
5 Petal-plucker's word
6 Greek marketplace
7 Shade of pink
8 Actress Celeste
9 Collection including Scandinavian myths
10 South American cowboy
11 Boston's Bobby
12 Bulk-food drawer
13 SSNs, e.g.
18 Carriers or cruisers, e.g.
19 Work the earth, in a way
23 German automaker
25 Tel ___
26 Golfer Ballesteros
27 ''Diamonds ___ Forever'' (1971)
29 Tankard brew
30 Some may be fine
31 Superman wears them
33 Hairstyle once worn with platform shoes
34 Churchillian gesture
36 Norse god of war
37 Shaving injury

38 Single
39 Tourist establishment
40 Mineral spring
43 Modifies
44 Chiromancer, e.g.
46 Suppresses
47 Run off without paying a debt
48 Decorator's choices
50 Late stand-up comedian Myron

51 Word with sing or string
54 Catches red-handed
55 Type of circus
56 Word with live or hot
57 Garner
58 Joanne Woodward title role
59 Born
60 Plum part

23

TAKEN TO THE CLEANERS

By Alice Walker

ACROSS

1 Untamed one
7 Vet's memory, perhaps
10 Lava lamps and such
14 To some extent
15 Aviation hero, e.g.
16 "___'Clock Jump"
17 Story setting, e.g.
18 Part of NASDAQ
20 The sky, to Atlas
21 Where a pitcher may rest
22 Equivalent of a pitcher's nod to the catcher
25 Oodles
26 DeLuise of comedy
28 "Odyssey" is one
30 Scribble aimlessly
34 Put-on
35 The merry widow in "The Merry Widow"
37 More factual
38 Take the show on the road
40 "Peachy keen!"
42 Genesis name
43 Part of a dying fire
45 Name of a noted sheep
47 Sugar amt.
48 Teeter-totter
50 Mentor in spiritual topics, perhaps
51 CEO's transport, perhaps
52 Theater prize
54 Clement Moore's "right jolly old elf"

56 Operating room apparel
60 Feedback of a sort
63 Speedy messengers
64 Type of apartment
66 Fuel cartel
67 Mix of oaters
68 Claim
69 Walk in up to the ankles
70 CIA precursor
71 Sat a spell

DOWN

1 Missile storage
2 Soon, bard-style
3 Old-time radio part
4 Covered
5 Square-dance partner, perhaps
6 Mr. Potato Head part
7 Zola novel
8 "... with ___ of thousands!"
9 System
10 Dog-tired from hiking, e.g.
11 Diva Moffo
12 One in Frank's Rat Pack
13 Word that closes the bidding
19 Comeback in a kids' argument
21 Yammered, e.g.
23 Beginning of "Nowhere Man"
24 Well-briefed about
26 Parts of history tests
27 Entreaty to "all ye faithful"

29 Hellos and goodbyes, Italian-style
31 Novel protection
32 Buy alternative
33 Emulate Dante's Peak
36 Finally
39 It can be drawn on
41 First name in Olympic gymnastics
44 Yeshiva leader
46 It's tender in Tokyo
49 Not taken in by

53 New currency on the Continent
55 Goes public
56 Garbage barge, e.g.
57 Manilow song setting
58 Felt repentant
59 Distinctive practices
61 Beyond large
62 Newspaper section
64 Kind of dance or bride
65 Ginger follower

MARCH ON
By Fran & Lou Sabin

ACROSS

1 Verbal elbow in the ribs
5 Join the rat race
9 Props for Chaplin
14 Asian housemaid
15 Infamous czar
16 "Island of the Blue Dolphins" author
17 Contraction with number one
18 Betting setting
19 ___ Jean (Marilyn Monroe)
20 March by 36-Across or a daily newspaper (with "The")
23 Abner's mother
24 It's a real mesh
25 Feeling concern
28 Min. fraction
29 Tierra ___ Fuego
32 Carpet layer's calculation
33 Completely inoperative
35 "Norma ___" (Sally Field film)
36 The March King
40 Boston-born Thurman
41 Thick, waterproof fabric
42 Statements in a pack?
43 Capture a crook
44 Common connector
45 Swim like a dog
47 Word with living or dead
48 Pie part
50 President's "theme song"
56 Superior to
57 Squeeze the Klaxon, e.g.
58 Ponder

60 Not as antiquated
61 Johnson of "Laugh-In"
62 Lake, city or canal
63 Tumbler
64 Sport
65 A kid might skip it

DOWN

1 Dad, in the boonies
2 Diving bird
3 Teasdale of poetry
4 He's in a cast
5 Switchboard innards
6 Some run on gas
7 Tall and slender
8 Stomach woe
9 Teaches a great class
10 Espouse
11 Emperor after Claudius
12 "Desire Under the ___"
13 Spline
21 Solo on film
22 A tie score
25 Certain Louisiana native
26 Food factor
27 Back-to-health process
28 "Wheel of Fortune" choice
29 Celtic priest
30 Meeting room prop, perhaps
31 Auto-dealership offer
33 Jason of the NBA
34 Quaffer's choice
37 Hothouse containers
38 John Wayne oater

39 Vet
45 Prepare to kiss (with "up")
46 Word with can or Wednesday
47 Diminutive beings of folklore
48 Errand
49 Oscar de la ___
50 Be suspended

51 Prototypical victim
52 Council Bluffs locale
53 Warming of relations
54 Currency abroad
55 Gymnast's feat
59 Shelter

MATERNAL INSTINCTS

By JoLene Andrews

ACROSS

1 Supergirl's City
5 Balloon
10 Places for pickles
14 Prefix meaning "skin"
15 Shoptalk
16 Words signifying trouble ahead
17 Quickly, quickly
18 Remove a tube top?
19 Joan Sutherland or Judi Dench, e.g.
20 Nobel Peace Prize winner of 1979
23 Have great faith in
24 Grinned from ear to ear
28 Word with Gatos or Altos
29 Really big singer?
32 "___ Sexy" (Right Said Fred tune)
35 Asian peninsula
36 "Well, ___-di-dah"
37 Sounds of pleasure
38 Al Capp's Pansy Yokum
39 Old-time wraparound
40 X-ray supplement
41 Fertile soils
42 Extend a subscription
43 House owner in a Martin Lawrence comedy
45 Lacking brightness
46 Term of respect in colonial India
47 Apollo's twin sister

51 Term of endearment
55 RE:
58 Cheese type
59 Run, but go nowhere
60 Fourth rock from the sun
61 It's for good measure
62 League constituent
63 Capital of Samoa
64 Like a flophouse
65 Sweet potato cousins

DOWN

1 Sixth U.S. president
2 Plant new crops
3 Frame of bars
4 Belly button
5 Some dust jacket paragraphs
6 Like a dryer's trap, typically
7 Start of many Grimm tales
8 Gelling agent
9 Lift one's spirits?
10 Like the laws of kosher food
11 "Now I get it!"
12 CD follower
13 That boat
21 Ending for switch or buck
22 Overwhelm with humor
25 Bird of prey's weapon
26 Application
27 "Balderdash!"
29 "___ Mia!"
30 Poor contributions?
31 What 5 can represent
32 Frost's feet?

33 Natalie Wood portrayal
34 Chicken portion
35 Title of respect
38 Maternal palindrome
39 Fearlessness
41 The gray wolf
42 "Educating ___" (Caine film)
44 Brunch beverage, perhaps
45 "Once upon a midnight ___
   ..."
47 Threw in
48 Euripedes tragedy
49 Sunni religion
50 Poppy supporters
52 Leaders in baseball, briefly
53 Pouty look
54 Season to be jolly
55 GPs' grp.
56 Vermont harvest
57 Prefix for pod

UNSEASONABLY WARM

By James Avery

ACROSS

1 Hatchet handle
5 Word in a Caldwell title
9 It puts the House on display
14 Popular cookie
15 Place for a dip
16 Palette pigment
17 It's kept in a reservation
19 Fictional Lorna
20 Thurman of films
21 Company in a 2000 merger
22 Like some sheets
23 Speak evil of
25 ''Quickly!''
27 Faddish adornment
29 Dot-___ (Internet company)
32 Basil-based sauce
35 Drinking binge
36 Tree trunk
37 Scarlett's mother
38 Word hidden in this puzzle's theme entries
39 Drop by
40 Singer/songwriter Young
41 Sound partner
42 Start of a Shakespeare title
43 Kind of mother
44 Like a liberal giver
46 Like family movies
48 Getting nowhere fast
52 Staircase parts
54 Affection, in brief
55 Santa trailer
56 Was audibly impressed

57 Out of touch with reality
60 Ben Franklin creation
61 Nightclub of song
62 Libretto
63 Gnawed away
64 WWII weapon
65 Hostelries

DOWN

1 Unexciting
2 It may waft
3 One's first position?
4 The third of three X's
5 Blacksmiths' wear
6 Nonchalant
7 Tigger's pal
8 Samara source
9 Writing a computer program
10 ''Ivanhoe'' author
11 Use a certain office machine
12 ''Comus'' composer
13 It's more than a desire
18 Gilligan's Island feature
22 Bowl for baptismal water
24 Chip producer
25 Looked over for errors
26 Violent demonstrator
28 Natural gas component
30 Collage
31 It's read at the table
32 Remain unsettled
33 ''Waiting for the Robert ___''
34 Biblical weapon
36 ___ nova

39 Potbelly
41 Play constructions
44 Arboretum, e.g.
45 "The Wizard of Oz" prop
47 "Superman" star
49 Implicate
50 Baseball players have one

51 Small fasteners
52 Wine choice
53 Jot or tittle, e.g.
54 Classification
57 Windows boxes?
58 Toper
59 Kimono accessory

THREE IN A ROW
By Kamy Shore

ACROSS
1 Sounds from the cote
5 About, in legalese
9 "Saturday Night Fever" milieu
14 Egyptian dancing girl
15 Exhaust
16 Rodrigo Diaz de Vivar
17 Cezanne specialty
19 Light-headed?
20 Hare's challenger
21 Follows a certain recipe direction
22 Wolf type
23 Oil container
24 Hem material
27 Place for a markdown
30 Clemency
31 Bread of the future
32 Actress Thurman
33 Turtle feature
34 Part of Miss Muffet's meal
35 Pull an all-nighter
36 Stalling-for-time sounds
37 Terpsichore's forte
38 Glowed
39 Scientific inquiry
41 Elbowroom
42 Baseball maneuver
43 Nuclear reactor part
44 Sums
46 Mao, for one
50 Giraffe relative
51 Challenge for some rock climbers

52 Come into existence
53 Charity distribution
54 Apartment
55 Great dogs
56 Word with crazy or fry
57 Calculator display components, for short

DOWN
1 Ligneous fiber
2 Like some singing
3 Arabian chieftain (Var.)
4 Deer-attracting deposit
5 In neutral
6 Serenity spoiler
7 Plentiful
8 Zurich-to-Munich dir.
9 Corrupt morally
10 "Maybe"
11 "Reversible Errors" author
12 Movie house, overseas
13 Equalizing allowance
18 Wacko
21 Places for drunken sailors
23 Unrefined
24 Glowing piece of coal
25 Tractor maker
26 Launderer's challenge
27 Swingers' place?
28 Kitchen appliance brand
29 Spoiled or tainted, as meat
31 Unflattering type of cap
34 Checks one's age
35 Pollyannaish

37 The Kansas City Star and
   Baltimore Sun, e.g.
38 Sans ___
40 Pass, as time
41 Slip-on shoe
43 Pepper that packs a punch
44 Type of stool

45 Gumbo ingredient
46 Coagulate
47 Lion's pride?
48 Kind of rock or rain
49 Butterfly catchers
51 Teen's collection

SALUTE
By April Daye

ACROSS

1 This puzzle's theme
5 Pusher pursuers
10 It wasn't built in a day
14 Warning sign
15 Here and there
16 Inter ___
17 Grain-field weed
18 Ditto
19 German philosopher Immanuel
20 Boardroom bigwigs
23 Coffee-to-go requirement
24 Perfect score for some
25 Sheriff's band
28 Radical '60s grp.
31 Visibly elated
35 "I ___ Camera" (1955 film)
36 Director's prerogative
39 Hercules' captive
40 Irritants for the boss
43 Chills and fever
44 More obsequious
45 Do-it-yourselfer's buy
46 Boutonniere's place
48 Russian-born writer Rand
49 Chooser's choice
51 First name among legendary crooners
53 Fr. holy woman
54 Superior recruit, e.g.
63 Bog
64 Stiller's spouse
65 Spectacular star

66 Poor Yorick's word
67 Start of a new book
68 Auricular
69 Utilize and return
70 Threesome
71 Armed forces option

DOWN

1 Campus military org.
2 Nanjing nursemaid
3 St. Philip
4 Shows subservience, in a way
5 Designated
6 Summit
7 Merit
8 Gator kin
9 Stocky
10 Words with profits or the dough
11 Norway's patron saint
12 Child's assertion
13 Truck-stop offerings
21 Tempestuous
22 Texas ___ (oil)
25 Like some bulls
26 The end, in the Bible
27 Stopped lying?
28 Thin narrow groove
29 Frequency of Baltimore's Sun
30 Yarn buy
32 English philosopher John
33 Vegetable-oil component
34 Adam and Mae
37 Kind of trip

38 Holiday forerunner
41 Most miniscule
42 Narrow mountain ridge
47 Fond du ___, Wis.
50 Mount of New York
52 Emulate Eden's serpent
53 Sedate
54 Tent tycoon

55 Smoothing tool
56 Kukla's lady
57 Target of a swift kick, perhaps
58 Wise men
59 Geometric measure
60 Scintilla
61 Tel follower
62 Like a bertha collar

FOWL BALL

By Alice Walker

ACROSS

1 ___ fide (in bad faith)
5 Not a good vibration?
10 Soon, in the past
14 Hutchinson and Gray
15 Big name in toy trucks
16 Italian city, to the Italians
17 Animated hit featuring Mel Gibson
19 Bowler's feature
20 "Great blue" bird
21 Welcome a new frat member, in a way
23 Opens up, as a drain
26 Go-___ (small racing vehicle)
27 Father's Day gifts, often
29 Wine bottle
33 Writer Kingsley
37 Hard journey
39 Insertion mark
40 Once-popular coiffure
43 Keep ___ on the ball
44 What linen is made from
45 Mentor of 36-Down
46 Pivotal Pacific battle of WWII
48 Largest organ
50 Between ports, e.g.
52 Quarantine
57 One criterion for an R rating
61 Investment firm Goldman ___
62 Out of control
63 Ragtime dance
66 Hawaiian state bird
67 Like the Leaning Tower of Pisa

68 Fork part
69 It twinkles
70 Appears to be
71 Borderline

DOWN

1 ___ Picchu, Peru
2 Drained of color
3 Hibernation locations
4 Old-fashioned tie
5 Sault ___ Marie
6 Long geological stretch
7 Crucifix inscription
8 Pepe Le Pew, for one
9 "Flashdance" hit song
10 Selected at random
11 Writer Ephron
12 Neglect to mention
13 It's on every driver's license
18 It may be tied in church
22 Bingham of "Baywatch"
24 Pocket sandwich bread
25 Sans ___ (print type)
28 Trades for money
30 With the bow, in music
31 Bitter quarrel between two families
32 R&B singer James
33 He had no mother
34 "Scarface" star Paul
35 One way to serve tea
36 Sci-fi hero created by George Lucas
38 Uniform material, sometimes

41 Add body to hair
42 X or y, e.g.
47 Blabbermouths
49 Overly curious
51 Kind of angle
53 Coffee-shop order
54 Bitter-tasting
55 Type of sandal or bikini

56 First name in cosmetics
57 Some small-business vehicles
58 ''___ Him on a Sunday''
59 Charlie Chaplin's last wife
60 Lake, city or canal
64 Airline to Amsterdam
65 Space invaders

EXECUTIVE PRODUCER

By Isaiah Burke

ACROSS

1 Look with malicious intent
5 Word to a pest
10 Commiserator's word
14 Advocate
15 Town in Greenland
16 Pilaf ingredient
17 What some climb
20 Sports drink suffix, perhaps
21 Step backward?
22 James or Owens
23 Some parlor pieces
25 Country singer Jackson
27 Denizen of a certain farm
28 Batting eyelids, licking lips, etc.
32 Beach find
35 Lavish celebration
36 Anonymous litigant
37 Worker's dream, perhaps
41 Poetic pugilist
42 It's in the pot
43 Opposite of sets
44 Doggedness
47 32,000 ounces
48 Tacit approvals
49 What the kittens lost
53 Pergola
56 Indian garment
57 Emulate a landscaper
58 Executive's parting gift
62 Fencer's weapon, sometimes
63 Lubricated
64 Locale of original sin

65 Keeps folks in stitches?
66 Skein components
67 Nuthatch home

DOWN

1 Skywalker's creator
2 Deteriorate, in a way
3 Wading bird
4 Bench press unit
5 Address part, often
6 Powwows
7 Road grooves
8 Brit's brew, perhaps
9 Bugs' voice
10 Impassioned
11 They're blown in anger
12 They're sometimes more important than kings
13 Without moisture
18 With candor
19 Slightly cracked
24 Statuesque
25 Jane Curtin role
26 One might be chronic
28 Kind of acid
29 Fateful day in March
30 What one little piggy had
31 Exacts revenge on
32 It may be reserved
33 Robust
34 "The Auld Sod," romantically
35 Well-bred Londoners
38 Speakeasy risk
39 Steamy

40 It's a real moneymaker
45 Battery terminals
46 Innermost part
47 Diatribe
49 Some equines
50 Dodge
51 What students pass
52 Exhausted

53 Years and years and years
54 You may skip it
55 Used a Breathalyzer
56 Shopper's delight
59 Eggy concoction
60 Exemplar of easiness
61 Brood tender

ANIMALS, FRONT AND BACK
By Edmond Rice

ACROSS

1 Fourth man
5 It may be 50 yards long
9 Horsewhip
13 Charley horse
14 They may be deserted
16 Maggie Simpson's sister
17 It feeds chiefly on plankton
19 Sainted king
20 Northern Europe adjective
21 Vamp's accessory, perhaps
22 Box office total
23 Unsightly citrus fruit?
25 Unlikely to cheat
27 It has a snoutlike trunk
31 Part of TGIF
32 It may turn
33 Strike location
37 Depleted
39 Fable offering
42 Within the group
43 Reaches across
45 Read electronically
47 Longstanding
48 It has a long prehensile tail
52 Call Cary Gary, e.g.
55 Simplicity
56 More than half of us are here
57 Breakfast of centurions?
59 Abalone abode
63 Manipulator
64 It's a hunting pooch
66 Olympic event
67 April 15th taxpayer, e.g.

68 First name in jazz
69 Place, as in a tourney
70 Forswear
71 Stop introducing evidence

DOWN

1 Cut, as a log
2 Sound effect
3 "___ she blows!"
4 Delayed
5 Renounce a legal claim to
6 Vesuvius output
7 Type of foundation
8 Sandwich shop offerings
9 A fleet of small craft
10 Whitman's dooryard bloomer
11 Large city of Japan
12 Auctioneer's tool
15 Pacific ray
18 Ice skating figure
24 ___-European (language family)
26 Chance occurrence
27 "Green ___ and Ham"
28 Grommet
29 Comedic Dame
30 To the point
34 Frenzied
35 Grouter's piece
36 Circular current
38 Caught in a trap
40 Farmland unit
41 Monastery of lamas
44 Relaxing retreat

46 Brown-___ (sycophant)
49 Parting words
50 Completely lacking
51 More within reach
52 Heavy hammers
53 Point in question

54 Military blockade
58 Wagon part
60 Ill temper
61 Morays, e.g.
62 "Curses, foiled again!"
65 Start of many countdowns

TAKE THE PLUNGE

By Alan Olschwang

ACROSS

1 Greek storyteller
6 Melville tale
10 Neighbor on
14 Word to the chauffeur
15 Entre ___ (between ourselves)
16 London district
17 Take the plunge
20 Seal in the juices
21 They may be pricked
22 River of forgetfulness
23 "Quickly!" acronym
25 Garbage pail on some desktops, e.g.
27 Take the plunge (with 49-Across)
31 Ivory or Coast, e.g.
35 The Marshall Islands, e.g.
36 Words with high standard
38 Wine label word
39 City on the Arkansas River
40 Unsers at Indy
41 Absolute, as nonsense
43 Old Tokyo
44 Unit of loudness
46 Euboea's locale
47 Spanish painter Jose Maria
49 See 27-Across
51 Suffix often denoting great wealth
53 Not aweather
54 Texas landmark
57 When King Lear disinherits Cordelia

59 "Bye-bye"
63 Take the plunge
66 "Rag Mop" brothers
67 Raise
68 Trunk item
69 Musical pause
70 Leftover morsels
71 Shimon of Israel

DOWN

1 Tallies
2 Canal of renown
3 Hindu religious figure
4 Farmer's garb, often
5 National Gallery East Building designer
6 Recorded
7 Tie up the tugboat
8 Exteriors
9 City near Tashkent
10 Trees with trembling leaves
11 Mukluk, for one
12 Apprehension expression
13 Enameled metalware
18 Approaches
19 "Xanadu" band
24 Rooms in Mexico
26 Portable place to sleep
27 Some are blind
28 Rachmaninoff piece
29 Decorator's decision
30 Lighthouse site, perhaps
32 Couple of quartets
33 Betel-nut source

34 Less contaminated
37 Halos
40 Termite terror
42 Send a wire
45 Rafter's need
46 Like the Arctic
48 Least wild
50 Misogynists, e.g.
52 Debtor's promise

54 Culture medium
55 Soil addition
56 Birds, to biologists
58 Fireside event
60 Not quite closed
61 Moved like lightning
62 Fortas and Lincoln
64 Paid player
65 Dangerous snake

ACROSS THE POND

By Kane Wesley

ACROSS

1 Chronological brinks
5 "Home Alone" kid
10 Chesapeake Bay catch, often
14 Feeling for the unfortunate
15 Don't exist
16 Tramp
17 Three-time U.S. Open champ Lendl
18 High-count fabric
20 Enormous
22 Agglomerate
23 Versifier
24 Phrase of insight
26 Melted-cheese dish
30 Graduates, briefly
33 Prefix meaning "sun"
34 Shakespeare title starter
35 Orchestra's place, sometimes
36 Epochs
37 Chevy
39 Hepcat talk
40 Fire preceder?
41 Starstruck trio?
42 More steamed
43 Hyson, e.g.
44 Part of the woodwind family
47 Tout's concerns
48 Element found in none
49 Utter boredom
52 One way to ride a horse
56 3M innovation
59 Caspian feeder
60 1855 Tennyson work

61 Entertainer Cheech
62 Currency in Pisa
63 Cube maker Rubik
64 Brief indulgence
65 After the bell

DOWN

1 Of majestic proportions
2 In ___ (occurring naturally)
3 Substitute for the unnamed
4 Summary
5 Type of roll
6 Literary errors
7 Sign of secrecy
8 Ones with the power
9 Ultimate, degreewise
10 Material for khakis
11 Part of The San Francisco Treat
12 Act as an accessory
13 Sacrum or parietal
19 Commits a deadly sin
21 London area
24 Qualified
25 Weapon handle
26 Bearded growth
27 Mysteriously spooky
28 Andes creature
29 Cooking herb
30 Richard's first veep
31 Missouri, Arkansas or Connecticut, e.g.
32 Uncompromising
37 Chicago or Boston, e.g.

1	2	3	4		5	6	7	8	9		10	11	12	13
14					15						16			
17					18					19				
20				21							22			
			23					24	25					
26	27	28					29					30	31	32
33							34					35		
36					37	38					39			
40				41						42				
43				44				45	46					
			47					48						
49	50	51					52					53	54	55
56					57	58						59		
60					61							62		
63					64							65		

38 They run only when broken
39 Typical English person
41 Combat doc
42 Nursery rhyme domicile
45 Where to find baked blackbirds
46 Unflustered
47 Surpass
49 Salinger dedicatee
50 State south of Va.
51 Subject, usually
52 Roseanne's maiden name
53 Callas solo
54 Dessert display place
55 Swiss painter, 1879-1940
57 Pinafore lead-in
58 Spigot

SCHOOL'S OUT

By JoLene Andrews

ACROSS

1 Vaulted church section
5 Hair curlers?
10 Rivers or Lunden
14 Rhythmic pulse
15 Bye-bye, in Burgundy
16 Take apart
17 Garb for a rite of passage
19 Unenviable grades
20 Skirt insert
21 Rather formal
23 Weather word
26 Toast topper
28 Wake-up calls
29 Bumper sticker phrase, usually
30 Advised leader?
33 Folder fodder
34 Salts, in a way
35 "The Cask of Amontillado" author
36 They're from Splitsville
37 Kind of dog
38 Horse sound
39 Mr. Caesar
40 "A Certain State of Mind" author Norma
41 Witchlike old woman
42 Prefix for corn or angle
43 Latin being
44 Boarding house occupant
45 Like all living organisms
47 Swift pieces
48 Japanese straw mat
50 ___ and crafts

51 Horror-film helper
52 When one becomes eligible for college
58 Weightlifting exercise
59 Mortal
60 China lead-in
61 Piano pieces?
62 League constituents
63 ___ out a living (scraped by)

DOWN

1 Start of a kindergarten song
2 Garbanzo, for one
3 Maple product
4 Places for knickknacks
5 National League team
6 Move bit by bit
7 Grande or Bravo
8 Feline sound
9 Like some raisins
10 Land occupied by Israel since 1967 (Var.)
11 What's obtained upon 52-Across
12 Lemon and lime drinks
13 Too inquisitive
18 Benchmarks
22 Dumbbell turns
23 Least dangerous
24 Word on a bottle of snake oil
25 Address at 52-Across
26 Raised to the second power
27 Runs smoothly, as an engine
31 Like some "tunes"

32 Biblical outcasts
34 Put the whammy on someone
37 Old-fashioned illumination
38 Transverse beam
40 Place to find leaders
41 Word with Rica or Mesa
44 "The Honeymooners"
   episodes, today
46 Countesses' counterparts

48 Watch sound
49 Feverish condition
50 First lady's man
53 Lament
54 "I ___ lineman for the county"
55 Media attention, in slang
56 Verse form
57 Say yes, in a way

I'M KNOWN FOR PUZZLES

By Gayle Dean

ACROSS

1 Guitar ridges
6 Brewing grain
10 Johnny's money?
14 Spine-tingling
15 Basin adjunct
16 Cognizant of
17 Skate's kin
18 He's known for his locker
20 She's known for her cow
22 Make rhapsodic
23 "To the max" indicator
24 Type of grease
25 It's a lock when pinned
26 Tiny colonizers
27 One of two needed for a score
28 The "O" in OTB
31 More bombastic
34 He's known for his mother
36 Hodgepodge
37 Escort of a sort
39 Established ceremony
40 He's known for a number
42 Like some cars and apartments
44 Equine has-been
45 Muumuu go-with
46 Polo participant
47 Ointments
49 Inventor of a '60s synthesizer
50 Whole amount
53 Colored marble
55 He's known for a code

57 He's known for revenge
59 Wheels of fortune?
60 Good way to have it
61 Lacking spirit
62 Site of thousands of flowers, perhaps
63 River through Opole
64 Type of club
65 Parts of some chairs

DOWN

1 ___ fatale
2 Brings up or things to bring up
3 Modern painter Max
4 Man who once stood behind Michael Jackson
5 Established water route
6 Chest decorations
7 Hardly oblivious
8 Conscript
9 "Old college" thing
10 Becomes less friendly
11 Capital near Chesapeake Bay
12 Printer's direction
13 It may go to blazes
19 Informal attire
21 Thrusts out
25 Valued, inherited possession
26 In awe
27 Word indexers often ignore
29 Wine and dine
30 Bedrock fellow
31 Homebuyer's need, often

32 Menlo Park name
33 Albuquerque's river
34 Doctor of sci-fi
35 Salver
38 Hindu title
41 "The Zoo Story" playwright
43 Inundates
46 Scented hair ointment
48 Complete

49 1950s first lady
50 Mead study site
51 Dangerous sub
52 Producers of sunbows
53 Short round?
54 Dare into doing
55 Pitch the horsehide
56 Streamlet
58 Veer suddenly

STAPLED

By Kenneth Drury

ACROSS

1 Ground cover
5 Some places to stay
9 Sales clerk's minimum
14 It starts in your head
15 Secluded place
16 Up to the time of
17 Far-fetched
18 Famous Amos
19 Hardly straight
20 Edible staples
23 Ad ___
24 What I may mean
25 Quote an authority
26 Interpretive dance, e.g.
27 Partners of cones
28 Gaiety
31 Adler of Sherlock Holmes stories
34 Is green around the gills
35 Nothing special
36 Edible staples
39 Flirtatious overture
40 State firmly
41 Warbucks, to Annie
42 Bug someone, e.g.
43 Ugandan despot
44 Word with horn or filter
45 Some lambs, someday
46 Graph ending
47 Restorative resort
50 Edible staples
54 Beautiful woman of paradise
55 Block found on a farm

56 Fabled underachiever
57 Own up to
58 Statements in a pack?
59 ___ mater
60 Genera
61 Start with while
62 Noted loch

DOWN

1 You can dig it
2 Pocatello locale
3 Archaeologist's quest
4 Powdery mineral
5 Desired outcome
6 Not you, I or them
7 She wrote about Harry and Sally
8 It determines black from white?
9 Peck's eight
10 Loosen, as a shoe
11 Related to the ear
12 Lay a floor
13 Computer key
21 "M*A*S*H" setting
22 Accomplished, biblically
26 Hill builders
27 Age
28 What you can't live without
29 Found a function for
30 Very inquisitive
31 Rapscallions
32 Gather from the fields
33 Desirable street?

34 Worthy of recommendation
35 Type of witness
37 Dubbed
38 Bye at the French Open?
43 Is pending
44 Ideally
45 Unsettling
46 Runs while sitting

47 Like yesterday's news
48 Head jobs?
49 Vicinities
50 Kind of language
51 Aitchbone locale
52 Depilatory brand
53 Common conjunction
54 Something to check

TOSSED ABOUT

By Kay Puttnam

ACROSS

1 Thrilling wheel
7 Pack down firmly
11 Tool of forensic science
14 Kindle
15 Spheroid do
16 Stadium ticket word
17 Part of the evening news
19 Kind of temper or wind
20 One of a maritime trio
21 Dullea of "2001: A Space Odyssey"
22 Word with mess or music
24 French seaport
26 Farmer's locale in song
27 D'amour leader
30 Biblical event
33 Shorthand system introduced in 1888
34 Bitter in taste
36 Word on a towel, perhaps
37 St. Petersburg river
38 Old floorboard sound
39 "No ifs, ands or ___!"
40 Private follower
41 Something to bring home
42 Ecuadorian currency, formerly
43 Road to conflict
45 Grow more profound, as a plot
47 Taprooms
48 Stand in the mall
49 Day many save for
51 Patrick's "Ghost" wife

52 Worm product
56 Gallery draw
57 Short distance
60 Often-bracketed bit of Latin
61 Rapt in reverence
62 Triumvirate
63 "Yeah, right!"
64 Edible tuber
65 Performs as a guest

DOWN

1 Babe in the woods
2 "... ___ saw Elba"
3 Horse with a gray-sprinkled coat
4 Swedish turnip
5 Suffix for bull or freak
6 Player in a kids' game
7 Unsaid but understood
8 Off in the distance
9 Homemaker's title, sometimes
10 Mint or thyme, e.g.
11 It'll hold a bit
12 Four-time Super Bowl-winning coach
13 If they're boring, they're doing their job
18 Kind of grant
23 Menu phrase
25 Highway hauler
26 Actor Bogarde
27 VP under Nixon
28 Norse love goddess
29 High degree of excitement

30 Intervening period
31 Petrol unit
32 Original Krupp Works city
35 VIP in business
38 Half of the pairs in a downpour?
39 Some ammunition
41 Helped out Mom and Dad, in a way
42 Spanish ayes
44 Groaner of a joke

46 Lifting devices
48 Japanese form of fencing
49 Poison ivy souvenir
50 Diva's specialty
51 Goldbrick's opposite
53 Flower of one's eye?
54 Mythical mischief-maker
55 Olympic skater Michelle
58 Howard Hughes once controlled it
59 Word form for "three"

TREMOR ALERT

By Kamy Shore

ACROSS

1 Southwestern land formation
5 Bring embarrassment to
10 It may bounce off walls
14 Loving son of myth
15 Word with truth or blood
16 More than relax
17 What happens during a tremor?
19 Ball brand
20 Edible root from the High Andes
21 Paul's partner, once and again
22 Places to go around in circles
23 Rock tour venue
25 Where to view the House?
28 What happens during a tremor?
33 Type of replay, briefly
35 Hardly a libertine
36 Sometimes it's for the money
37 "___ it going?"
38 Brings in the harvest
39 Snowballed
40 Kwan's surface
41 Swindling scheme
42 Twelfth anniversary gift
43 What happens during a tremor?
46 Drawing of interest to many
47 Contraction with enough or entertainment
49 Object of frequent sightings

52 Half a ballroom dance
53 Popular tower?
55 Biennial vegetable
56 What happens during a tremor?
60 1998 animated film
61 Center of Miami
62 Bias
63 Minding everyone else's business
64 Sounds of impatience
65 Salinger dedicatee

DOWN

1 Reminder
2 Novelist Jong
3 Type of energy
4 Stop wondering, perhaps
5 Guru's retreat
6 Ready for the sack
7 Ham's shelter, for a time
8 Ambulance chaser's advice
9 Letters at sea
10 Weather's bad boy
11 Ethan or Joel of movies
12 "Listen!"
13 Tip or rip finish
18 Panasonic rival
22 Beefsteak order, sometimes
24 Boulevard liners, sometimes
25 Orange-flavored liqueur
26 Tosspot's state
27 Third degrees
29 Words to a gift recipient

30 They're all ears, practically
31 It's capped and may be slapped
32 Put in stitches
33 Thug's blade
34 Graph points
38 Litter's littlest
39 Type of monster
41 Life stories, briefly
42 "The Merry Widow" composer
44 Pretentiously showy

45 Some alcohols
48 City of witch hunts
49 Abba of Israel
50 Jay seen at night
51 Seasoned hands
52 Show appreciation, in a way
54 "... long ___ both shall live"
56 Psalms preceder
57 112.5 degrees away from S
58 "Jungle Fever" director
59 Sugary suffix

FROM STATE TO STATE

By April Daye

ACROSS

1 Stimulates
6 One way to hide a present
10 Church section, perhaps
14 Honor a loan
15 Rodentlike mammal
16 Give two thumbs up
17 Conversation opener
19 Recipe qtys.
20 Rational
21 Insignificant speck
22 Plaint for Billie Joe
23 Bart's grandpa
24 19th in a Greek series
26 Monopoly quartet (Abbr.)
28 Much-loathed emperor
30 Obtains with effort
32 Friend abroad
33 Pie-mode connector
36 Table protector
38 Cottonmouth
41 Type of vinegar
42 Seventh Greek letter
43 Add'l phone line
44 State or city in India
46 Instinctive motive
50 Transcript stat.
51 Tokyo, once
52 Whipped cream unit
55 It merged with Time Warner
56 Part of U.S.A.
58 First name in boxing
60 Second word in a fairy tale
61 Cafeteria feature, perhaps

63 Repair
64 Actor Penn
65 Immigration Museum island
66 They may be liberal
67 Bubkes
68 Frozen raindrops

DOWN

1 Where "Don Quixote" was conceived
2 Become more distant
3 Show's first number
4 Applies with a cotton swab, e.g.
5 Part of the Fertile Crescent
6 Pequod, for one
7 Not leave leaves
8 Something I can't use, but you can
9 Word with diem or capita
10 Countertenor
11 Deli order
12 Seinfeld's comic book hero
13 Actors Asner and Harris
18 Wane
21 Capital on the Gulf of Oman
24 Soft end of the Mohs scale
25 With celerity
27 Command to a guest
29 Mare fare
31 Miocene, for one
34 Beginning of a cassette tape
35 Partner of dangerous
37 Levi's uncle

38 Aluminum foil alternative
39 Rock concert site chronicled in "Gimme Shelter"
40 "Venus de ___"
41 Ask, in an undignified way
45 Lizard in a Tennessee Williams title
47 Walk or talk aimlessly
48 Certain hockey player
49 Firstborn

53 Electrical resistance unit
54 Famous film motel
57 These might be split
58 "Coming of Age in Samoa" author
59 Anchor store locale
60 Thurman of "Batman & Robin"
61 Taxpayer's ID
62 Mad Hatter's drink

ABOVE IT ALL

By Alice Walker

ACROSS

1 Places for coats
5 Songdom's pistol packer
9 "Achilles and the Tortoise" subject Mark
14 Algerian port
15 Poetic pronoun
16 Carrot-top creator
17 Doris Day comedy
20 "Bye," somewhere
21 Posted
22 Great lack
24 Green sage of film
25 Short trip
28 Subj. for immigrants, perhaps
29 Apply with a swab
31 North American capital
33 Word in a Christmas carol title
36 Ship's frame
37 One way to be in love
41 Chicken style
42 Petty officer
43 Assert without proof
46 Don'ts partner
47 Sculptor's leaf, perhaps
50 Rocky's greetings
51 Easy-to-grow houseplant
54 Tristram Shandy creator
56 Pulled vehicle
58 Argentine first lady
59 Richard Dreyfuss comedy
63 Walking ___ (elated)
64 Abound

65 German's neighbor
66 "The Divine Miss M"
67 Bit of progress
68 Got a load of

DOWN

1 Scented hair ointment
2 Wears down
3 Crocodile kin
4 Unwelcome look
5 Music channel
6 Polite interrupter
7 Snakelike tropical swimmer
8 Sound on the air
9 Thug's message
10 Merge metals
11 "Wheel of Fortune" buy, perhaps
12 Keeper's charge
13 Faultfinder
18 Surpassed
19 Tough-guy actor Ray
23 Angelic ring
25 Transport, as freight
26 They fly by night
27 Sidekick
30 Group of people, animals or things
32 And so
33 Use a piggy bank
34 Maiden name intro
35 Walked heavily
37 Hawaiian city
38 Snakelike fishes

39 Some medical grps.
40 Day for bonnets
41 Bandleader Kyser
44 In abundance
45 Ht.
47 Sergeant with badge 714
48 Chant
49 Made to mesh
52 "Golden Boy" playwright

53 White-plumed bird, often
55 Sidestep
56 State of irritation
57 Fencing blade
59 Type of scene
60 Bottom of some scales
61 Meal starter?
62 It helps pump up the volume

SCARY PEOPLE
By Kane Wesley

ACROSS

1 Frankenstein's gofer
5 Kitchen piece, perhaps
10 Turkish leader
14 Nonnegotiable item
15 German sub
16 Broadway production
17 Actor in scary roles
19 Bring down the house?
20 Were now?
21 Hale and Ladd
22 Lies low
23 Uninvited partygoer
25 Where Singaraja is
26 Kiss partner
27 Exclude from practice
30 Mythical monster
33 Suffix with patriot or manner
36 Like a sacker of Rome
38 Actor in scary roles
42 An alarm clock or rooster, e.g.
43 Photo ___ (camera sessions)
44 Track act
45 Underground growth
47 Norwegian metropolis
51 Package delivery org.
53 Hunting dog
56 "West Side Story" song
58 Items in a hold
60 Tasteless newspaper
61 Country on the Caspian
62 Actor in scary roles
64 After-bath powder, perhaps

65 Mountain ridge
66 ___ fixe
67 "Will there be anything ___?"
68 Editor's marks
69 Kevin Costner role

DOWN

1 Strike forcefully
2 Nom de ___ (pseudonym)
3 Pertaining to bone
4 66 is a well-known one (Abbr.)
5 Bridal veil material, perhaps
6 On the train
7 Brought into the world
8 Phyllis' never-seen TV husband
9 Summer on the Cote d'Azur
10 Clock-changing month
11 Sword lilies
12 It follows "Purple" in a song title
13 Seafaring assents
18 Preppy cheer
22 In great need
24 Smooth and glossy
25 Stringed instrument
28 Tennis legend Chris
29 Chesapeake, for one
31 Brazilian vacation destination, for short
32 "Proud Mary" grp.
34 Tibetan guide
35 Spanish hands
37 Williams of "Happy Days"

38 Scientist's site
39 Be obligated to
40 Seven and eleven, in Vegas
41 Classical prefix
46 "Doctor at Large" character
48 Walked with a purpose
49 Rental agreements
50 Saturnalias
52 From a time

54 Leers at
55 Promissory note
56 Wee parasite
57 Asian sea
58 Dick Francis book "Dead ___"
59 Away from the wind
62 Some university degs.
63 Jubilant cry in a card game

MINUTE BY MINUTE
By JoLene Andrews

ACROSS
1 Sweater letter, perhaps
5 Dust movers
9 Antiquated old times
13 Substitute for the unnamed, briefly
14 Egg without a shell
15 Singer Ross
17 Invisible quality
18 Horologes
20 Interpret speech without hearing
22 Inc.'s kin
23 With it
24 Rendezvoused
25 Vagabonds' transportation, maybe
27 Signal that danger has passed
31 Kabibble of Kay Kyser's band
32 Prepares water for JELL-O
33 Word with shoe or bull
35 They may be found in labs
39 Gabrielle Chanel's nickname
40 Cock and bull
41 Concerto instrument
42 Something to build on?
43 Footnote abbr.
44 Not active
45 Cognizance
47 Eats
49 Farm laborers of low social rank
53 Objective
54 Turnstile part
55 ___ Locks (Sault Ste. Marie Canal)
56 States categorically
60 Common accessory
63 Historic Irish village
64 River of Hades
65 Throw down the gauntlet
66 Son of Seth
67 Batik artisan
68 Institutes legal proceedings against
69 Purges

DOWN
1 Ardor
2 Holder of combs, perfumes, etc.
3 Infield covering
4 Sleep enders
5 Turn about
6 Voracious
7 Wrigley field?
8 Something in a trash heap
9 Formal decrees
10 Tell it like it isn't
11 Home on the Black Sea, perhaps
12 Scrooge's expression
16 Egyptian cobras
19 Steppes
21 Snakelike fish
25 Romps playfully
26 Ship's clock
27 Fundamentals

28 Airplane maneuver
29 Parasitic insects
30 Gregory Peck role of 1956
34 Give a face-lift to
36 Already retired
37 Burned rubber
38 Defeats a bidder
40 Jonas Grumby's ship
44 Freesia's relative
46 Parade day
48 Spates

49 Ratchet catch
50 Was wrong
51 Peaceful relations
52 Prince Charming wannabes
56 Port near Haifa
57 Wife of a rajah
58 Hoofed it
59 Impudent talk
61 Adventure novel of 1887
62 19th Greek letter

63

EXTRACTING DATA

By George Keller

ACROSS

1 Thesaurus name
6 Leave unchanged, to an editor
10 Read quickly
14 Sleep disorder
15 Underground chamber
16 Remove an outer coating
17 Movie with a very sad ending
19 China placement?
20 Planning to vote no
21 Left Bank locale
22 "Are you serious?"
23 Like Lewis Carroll's oysters
25 Golf trap contents
27 Hullabaloo
30 Horror film with rats
31 "Dear old" one
32 You can take it or beat it
35 Founder of modern chemistry
38 Abu ___
40 "The Life of Riley" character
41 Word in a social register, perhaps
42 Davenport denizen
43 Mass of humanity
44 Most vitreous
46 Flue residue
47 Elmira locale, for short
49 17th Greek letter
50 Legal matter
51 Length X width
53 Property encumbrances
55 Pivot
57 German poet Heinrich

59 Give the heave-ho
63 Aerated drink
64 Wheeler-dealer
66 Still under cover
67 Memorable periods in history
68 Island of central Hawaii
69 Portend
70 Infamous Spandau prison inmate
71 Mine vehicles

DOWN

1 Pro ___ (in proportion)
2 Ready for business
3 Buzzing annoyance
4 Like a Stephen King story
5 ___ Mahal
6 Movie presentations
7 Oxlike Asian climber
8 Tied
9 Mother ___ (Nobel Peace Prize winner)
10 Engender
11 Teller's charge
12 Opera solo
13 With no ice
18 Bass-baritone Simon
24 Texas city
26 "Cato" playwright
27 See you in Hawaii?
28 Rectangular grooves
29 Made extensive revisions to
31 Dismal state
33 Demean

34 Ice cream units
36 Ancient
37 Conger, e.g.
39 Polloi lead-in
45 Wool source
48 A name of God
52 "The Cloister and the Hearth" author
53 Bygone coins

54 Word with system or battery
55 Strikebreaker
56 Timber wolf
58 Land of the leprechauns
60 Elbow-wrist connecting bone
61 Line for a sewer?
62 Speaker of baseball
65 To the max, for short

WHAT THEY DO

By Kane Wesley

ACROSS

1 Hides the gray, in a way
5 It follows larval
10 Comedian Sahl
14 Work hard for
15 Gracefully athletic
16 Winged
17 What a private may do
20 "___ Less Ordinary" (1997 film)
21 Certain bird shelter
22 Armed forces branch, briefly
25 Japanese capital
26 Mushroom part
29 One jumping through hoops
31 Hearing and smell
36 Secondhand
38 They're part of a good deal, usually
40 Colorful fish
41 What NASA employees may do
44 Fireplace rod
45 Just made (with "out")
46 Dreaded class word
47 Resembling a phonograph needle
49 Successful pitch result
51 Hemingway title word
52 Positive answer
54 Fred of "Sanford and Son"
56 Makes it to the top
61 Cruise destination, sometimes

65 What a mob accountant may do
68 Actor Bogarde
69 Serve the purpose
70 Muse count
71 One partner?
72 What a library does
73 Split personalities?

DOWN

1 Prefix meaning "ten"
2 You and you, down South
3 Part of a famous palindrome
4 Fly in the ointment
5 One way to stand
6 Cry of revulsion
7 Like the piper in Hamelin
8 Brass or bronze, e.g.
9 Goes
10 Cleopatra's love
11 Salmagundi
12 Rave partner
13 Trap, as a raccoon
18 Capone nemesis
19 Beliefs
23 Entree item, often
24 Secret stash
26 Tooth parts
27 Race site since 1711
28 Chipper
30 Vichyssoise veggies
32 Digs of twigs
33 Filthy places
34 Notched, as a leaf

The crossword grid (numbered cells):

1	2	3	4		5	6	7	8	9		10	11	12	13
14					15						16			
17			18					19					
20						21							
		22		23	24		25						
26	27	28		29			30		31		32	33	34	35
36			37		38			39		40			
41				42					43				
44					45					46			
47				48		49			50		51		
			52		53		54			55			
56	57	58	59				60			61		62	63	64
65						66	67					
68					69					70			
71					72					73			

35 One with a small work force
37 Quarrel settler of yore
39 Drag through the mud
42 Sounded like a donkey
43 Run, but go nowhere
48 Disclose
50 Red-clad cheese
53 Start the tennis game
55 It has no sting
56 Fashion magnate Gucci

57 First felon
58 Violent throw
59 Like cuttlefish defenses
60 Ollie's sidekick
62 Windows alternative
63 Nota ___ (take notice)
64 Yeoman's affirmatives
66 Evaded the seeker
67 Trains overhead

BREW CREW

By Thomas Hollingsworth

ACROSS

1 Beseeches
5 Makes a lot out of a building?
10 Figurine material, perhaps
14 Work as a barker
15 Tomato blight
16 Solemnly swear
17 Like some confessions
18 Large-eyed nocturnal primate
19 It has jaws but does not eat
20 They are reached for at many breakfasts
22 Suffixes for some citrus quaffs
23 Industrial container
24 Print measures
26 Restaurant of song
30 Calculate in advance
35 Banks once on the runway
36 Okla. city
38 Richie hit
39 It's on the house
40 MLB commissioner
42 Word with teen or matinee
43 Word with city or circle
45 Away from the weather
46 Kind of dream
47 Commits a criminal offense
49 Babble
51 Start for corn
52 General address?
53 Poker action
56 Starbucks offering
63 "O mio babbino caro," for one

64 Metric weight units
65 Telltale sign
66 Hector Hugh Munro
67 Draw forth
68 Cosmetic plant
69 More than promote criminal activity
70 Some Chippendales
71 It helps you focus

DOWN

1 Common-interest group
2 Prefix with bond or dollar
3 Seven-time Wimbledon champ
4 Word with taught or effacing
5 Discharges
6 Ratify
7 Mayan mathematical innovation
8 Give off
9 Back-talker
10 Programming language
11 Dyed-in-the-wool
12 Prescribed amount
13 Barnyard belles
21 Day before
25 "The" place for opera
26 Heart chambers
27 City on the Saone and Rhone
28 Clubs for Couples
29 It may be served with beignets
30 Occupies completely
31 Garfield's pal
32 Embezzler's worry

1	2	3	4		5	6	7	8	9		10	11	12	13
14					15						16			
17					18						19			
20				21							22			
				23					24	25				
26	27	28	29				30	31				32	33	34
35					36	37				38				
39					40				41		42			
43				44		45					46			
47					48				49	50				
			51					52						
53	54	55			56	57	58				59	60	61	62
63					64						65			
66					67						68			
69					70						71			

33 Sledding setting
34 President who married while in office
37 Spiffy
41 Many Mensa members
44 Perform a cowardly act
48 Like a defeated sucker?
50 Bow-shaped line
52 Memorable Vulcan

53 Home for la familia
54 Part of U.A.E.
55 Admire
57 White House staffer
58 Adding machine key
59 Shade of black
60 At rest
61 When some hear a whistle
62 Mine finds

SIGN OF THE TIMES
By Mark Milhet

ACROSS

1 Org. kin
5 Road scholar's book?
10 Methane's lack
14 Start of a Langston Hughes title
15 Where Kent went for a change?
16 Temp's pad
17 "Heaven Can Wait" actress Cannon
18 Impaneled one
19 Commiserator's word
20 Two times?
23 Miniver, for one
24 Princess's annoyance, in fable
25 Lassie, for one
29 Roman goddess
31 Type of tray
34 Situated between poles
35 Quaintly attractive
36 Percussion instrument
37 Three times?
40 You're tense on this
41 Wealthy
42 Language for the masses?
43 Part of WYSIWYG
44 First word in a Melville title
45 Map's table
46 Kind of pill or rally
47 Water temperature gauge, sometimes
48 Four times?
57 Sinister

58 Rustic abode
59 The life of Riley
60 Monthly expense, for many
61 When penitents convene?
62 National League stadium
63 Mine finds
64 One who avoids others
65 Bulgarian's neighbor

DOWN

1 Adjutant
2 Mythological river
3 Cleansing bar
4 "___ Nanette"
5 Renounce formally
6 Guided trips
7 Traditional knowledge
8 It's a little matter
9 Shell fragments
10 Cornhusker State hub
11 Sandwich shop
12 Muscat locale
13 Table wine
21 Dimple maker
22 Company exec.
25 Wear for Batman and Robin
26 Word with zinc or nitrous
27 Feudal superior
28 "Arsenic and Old ___"
29 Titillating
30 Mormon base
31 More than peeved
32 Aromatic seed
33 Correct text

35 Where baby sleeps
36 Word with race or queen
38 Caribbean climate
39 Baseball card manufacturer
44 Singer Torme
45 Car given as a temporary replacement
46 Trapper's collection
47 Lightweight cord

48 Cold reading
49 Word with throw or turn
50 Midmorning
51 Int'l org. formed in 1949
52 Deep black
53 Nuisance
54 Hawaiian island
55 Consumer
56 Shipbuilding wood

LET'S HAVE SOME PUN

By Edmond Rice

ACROSS

1 Smudged with soot
5 "... darkness ___ ignorance" (Luther)
10 Steals, ironically
14 Pope, 440-461
15 Actress Della
16 Region
17 Gathering of the brass?
20 Malleolus locale
21 Backslides
22 Hounds for payment
25 Feather partner
26 Victrola manufacturer
29 Fish, gerbils and such
31 Reduce speed
36 Instruments of war
38 Last word from Kasparov?
40 Squashed circles
41 Composer's liquor amount?
44 Permeate
45 Residential overhang
46 Part of Doris Day's theme song
47 Extremely poisonous
49 Idler's antithesis
51 Like the seafood in sushi, often
52 Place for a baby, at times
54 "It seemed like a good ___ at the time!"
56 Places of instruction and learning
61 Specialized vocabulary

65 Water sources in Denver?
68 Items in a smokehouse, perhaps
69 Half of Hispaniola
70 Poet Teasdale
71 What, who, how or where follower
72 Haggard hero Quatermain
73 Decorative pitcher

DOWN

1 Pond plant
2 "As ___ on TV!"
3 Respond to a bumper sticker, perhaps
4 Output
5 It's there for support
6 Serpentine swimmer
7 Paraphernalia
8 It's a good thing
9 Units of magnetic flux density
10 David, for one
11 Eyes, poetically
12 Soccer great
13 Verbalizes
18 Enlist again
19 Words between John Montagu and Sandwich
23 Verne captain
24 Barrel strip
26 More than zealous
27 ___ de menthe
28 Single-celled organism (Var.)
30 Word with in or home

32 Sheep
33 Thin, crisp biscuit
34 Sound beginning
35 "Fiddle-faddle!"
37 Small earring
39 Short stanza concluding a poem
42 "Catch-22" author Joseph
43 It needs room to grow
48 Honda rival
50 Derriere
53 Gas or clutch

55 Crop up
56 Muscle malady
57 Barbecue material
58 Gifts for the poor
59 Medicinal quantity
60 Growing medium
62 Chew on, as a bone
63 Fairy-tale villain
64 Peter or Ivan, e.g.
66 Depot (Abbr.)
67 Wrestler's goal

HANDY MATTERS

By George King

ACROSS

1 Cary Grant, originally
6 Man of many parts
11 Noisy dispute
14 Golf rarity
15 Piece of the pie
16 Commit a faux pas, e.g.
17 Old hands in the garden
19 Citrus suffix
20 Peak in the mythical war of the Giants
21 Plot set in the suburbs?
22 Comedian DeGeneres
24 Cooperstown's Ryan
26 ''Brian's Song'' character
27 Goon's blow-enhancers
31 Put down in writing?
32 Luau dish
33 Resign (with ''down'')
36 Kind of wind
37 Simpleton
40 Kooky
42 Glamorous Gardner
43 Defendant's part of the bargain?
45 Its floor is wet
47 Warren or Joyce Carol
49 Worst one to handle packages
53 Type of doll
55 Martini's partner
56 Pearl Mosque country
57 Guilty party, to a cop
58 Word oft shouted downtown

62 Prefix with ode or pod
63 Sign of nerves
66 Naval agreement?
67 Yankees skipper
68 One way to be lost
69 Was in front
70 Geisel's pen name
71 Daft

DOWN

1 Block brand
2 Cornstalk features
3 Seemingly forever
4 Purge
5 Mother ptarmigan
6 School of painters, c. 1908
7 Roil
8 Far from shocking
9 Spheroid
10 Put the lid back on
11 Houses and land
12 Court call
13 Some birds
18 Radio format
23 Caustic soaps
25 Christiania, today
26 Crash prelude, often
27 Radar sighting
28 Small brook
29 Physically fit
30 Make baby sounds
34 At any time
35 Third-and-long option
38 Concerning

39 Service charge
41 Gangland bigwigs
44 Their logo has four rings
46 Unpaid debts
48 Excitedly, in music
50 Champagne salutes
51 Long suits
52 Cosby TV series
53 Absolutely necessary
54 Deli phrase
57 Cole Porter's birthplace
59 Furthermore
60 Comic-book superheroes
61 Brit's exclamation
64 Tribulation
65 Chum

TIMES SQUARE

By April Daye

ACROSS

1 Black beef cattle
6 Defeat handily
10 Certain horses
14 Bounded
15 You may get a hand here
16 Succulent plant
17 Neighbor of Fiji
18 Oil port
19 Subject, usually
20 December 25, in a way?
22 They have their orders
23 Ancient alphabetic characters
24 Counterbalance, financially
25 "What ___ up must come down"
29 Word-breaker
31 Removes a bottle cap, perhaps
33 Saudi Arabian capital
37 Gives consent
38 Legendary siren
39 Try again, as a court case
40 So-so
41 Fermi's field
43 All bets are off after this
44 Right of final decision
47 Women's formal wear
49 Unpleasant thing to eat
50 May description, in a song
55 Flirtatious stare
56 ___ Major
57 Brick made of clay and straw
58 One of the Gospels

59 Brit's bit (of tea)
60 Broadcast more than once
61 Office furniture
62 Sound upstairs
63 Ivans IV and V, e.g.

DOWN

1 Moreover
2 Type of tide
3 Clue or backgammon, e.g.
4 Well-briefed about
5 Riser plus tread
6 Some police tactics
7 Shows bashfulness, in a way
8 Malaise
9 Skeletal
10 Unusually good 365 days
11 Audibly
12 In one's salad days
13 Have a hunch
21 The baby's room
24 Some whodunit suspects
25 Plant that makes gum
26 It's enough for some
27 Permanently mark
28 Important seven-day TV ratings period
30 In a coarse manner
32 43rd state
34 Goya's "The Duchess of ___"
35 Sandwich shop
36 Went in haste
38 Tear jaggedly
40 "A Star Is Born" director

42 Tibetan guide
44 Reprimand
45 Debate
46 Egg parts
48 Eligible for Mensa

50 Make messy or untidy
51 Poems of praise
52 One of Asta's owners
53 Skier's conveyance
54 Brood overseers

PART-TIMERS

By Kane Wesley

ACROSS

1 Pack animals
6 Vegetarian's option
10 Meat package letters
14 Legal setting
15 Cohesive entity
16 Calculator button
17 Part-time job, for some
19 Spew fire and brimstone
20 Rope in
21 Sharp end?
23 Word with ready, self or man
25 Stock-acquisition aid?
26 Employee in Siam, once
30 Bears' Field
33 Realty document
35 Facts and figures
36 Waikiki welcome
39 Part-time job, for some
43 It's fit for a pig
44 Procrastinator's opposite
45 "The Wild Swans at Coole" poet
46 Dresses for the cold (with "up")
49 Lazy Susan, essentially
50 Run the meeting
53 Tibetan creatures
55 Rues
58 Place firmly
63 Children's author Blyton
64 Part-time job, for some
66 First name in detective fiction
67 With bated breath
68 Aired anew
69 Tannery employee
70 Defaulted auto, perhaps
71 Ten in two, in an alley

DOWN

1 It's at the top of the heap
2 Any time now
3 Yukon and Tahoe, for two
4 "___ go bragh"
5 Power source for Fulton
6 It's often rented
7 Windsor's prov.
8 Some pre-Christmas purchases
9 Part of America
10 Brouhaha
11 Bed boards
12 Saharan sights
13 Cardinal competitor
18 Some timeline divisions
22 Chicago fire name
24 Eighty-something, e.g.
26 Donations
27 Not on the rocks
28 Not one, in Dogpatch
29 Start of a Faulkner title
31 German article
32 Meteor chaser?
34 Stand the test of time
36 Misinformant
37 Spanish 101 verb form
38 ___-bitsy
40 Billion-year stretch
41 Checkers side

42 Boxer's doc
46 Ornithologist
47 Half of carefree phrase
48 Snow transportation
50 Apollo in "Rocky"
51 This Brit made heads roll
52 Not awkward
54 Uses a swizzle stick

56 Lift at Aspen
57 Wise guy
59 El Paso campus, briefly
60 Gillette razor brand
61 Object of sadness
62 White-tailed sea eagle
65 Jazz style

VEGGIE'S DELIGHT

By Lynn Lempel

ACROSS

1 A la ___
6 Crush grapes, in a way
11 Tango requirement
14 Spacious window
15 Paramecium propellers
16 Divest
17 Versailles agreement, e.g.
19 Fuss
20 Campaigned
21 Commands to horses
22 Asocial type
24 Nimble Fred
26 Some revolve
28 Certain collectors' items
32 Barn bundles
35 Can't do without
36 "... ___ I saw Elba"
37 Pretty penny
38 Tea storage unit
40 What broken bones do when healing
41 ___ up (accelerate)
42 Good chunk of Mongolia
43 Some are blind
44 Comical GI
48 Like some eyes
49 Highway nuisances
53 Xenophobe's fear
55 "The Mocker Mocked" painter
56 Stand-up shtick
57 Result of a diplomacy failure, sometimes

58 Foundation
62 Furthermore
63 Once-popular anesthetic
64 Rib
65 "I've Seen All Good People" band
66 Stores
67 Stuffed

DOWN

1 The dried meat of the coconut
2 Some geometric findings
3 Pleasingly mirthful
4 Gumshoe
5 Mournful poems
6 Bug repellent, of a sort
7 Connections
8 Ending for pay or can
9 Harvard neighbor, popularly
10 Rocket's cargo
11 Fly-by-night
12 Shoe specification
13 Sulfur attribute
18 Prefix meaning "trillion"
23 Globe, e.g.
25 Support the scofflaw
26 Closing document
27 Follow orders
29 Kipling's homeland
30 Strange-sounding waterway?
31 Studio structures
32 Cutting remark
33 Toward shelter
34 Sweethearts or some parrots

38 Admitting both sexes
39 Noted advice dispenser
40 Clobber convincingly
42 Some are stolen
43 Loathes
45 Golfer's prop
46 Slackers and loafers, e.g.
47 Impolite look
50 It tried to avoid charges?

51 Dentist's direction
52 Mount for Lancelot
53 Far partner
54 Girlfriend for Kent
55 Was acquainted with
59 Hall of Famer Mel
60 Pi-sigma connection
61 Hyson, for one

CARPENTER'S HELPERS
By Carl Cranby

ACROSS

1 Floats gently
6 Word with down or out
10 Calais cleric
14 They're sometimes split
15 Woody's offspring
16 Casting requirement?
17 Heraldic borders
18 Precision marching group
20 Slowly permeate
21 Perrins' partner
22 Scottish landowners
23 Lose star status
25 Wild-boar features
27 Kind of donor
30 Guiding beliefs of a group
34 Mule of song
35 Bellini opera
36 Word with for or white
37 Piece on earth?
38 Terminus
39 Aunt of Andy
42 Jilted woman's comment of disgust?
43 Singing brothers
45 Brilliant success
47 Old TV "Squad"
48 Sticks in the mud
50 Sentry's attribute
52 Seating request
54 Offensive expression
55 Loofah, e.g.
58 Word with one or way
60 "Pygmalion" playwright

63 It precedes a laugh
65 Shorthand pro
66 Johnson of "Laugh-In"
67 Deprivation
68 Make giddy with delight
69 Old Oldsmobile competitors
70 Files litigation
71 Surrenders, formally

DOWN

1 "___ Sorry Now?"
2 River through Bern
3 Office supply item
4 Boring tool
5 Serpent's sound
6 Use hip boots
7 Printing mistake
8 Clay, once
9 Silver Ghost, informally
10 Agent's clientele, perhaps
11 Kind of belly
12 Strung item
13 Some street liners
19 Superior, for one
21 Bar twist
24 Unit of force
26 In functioning condition
27 State in northeast India
28 Country's Judd
29 Harrowing experience
31 Threat at sea
32 Butter substitutes
33 Faxes, e.g.
40 "... and ___ to rise ..."

82

41 Major ending
44 Roundtable sessions
46 Disinfect
49 Audible breath
51 Position comfortably
53 Auctions off, e.g.
55 Practice with a pug

56 Chaste
57 Logical beginning?
59 Legendary loch
61 Early bet
62 Serious troubles
64 Promissory note
65 Not as dry as brut

AREN'T YOU SWEET?

By Thomas Hollingsworth

ACROSS

1 Spanish munchies
6 Vegetable or tomato, e.g.
10 Industry magnate
14 Come up
15 Lhasa ___
16 Memorable Robinson role
17 Patty of "Peanuts"
19 Some queens, e.g.
20 67.5 degrees, to mariners
21 Unspecified amount
22 Italian bowling game
24 Spanky and the gang
26 Company car, e.g.
27 Screech, for one
28 Varieties of nuts
32 Super Bowl V winners
35 Pick the pick of the litter, e.g.
36 Prefix follower
37 Item of finality in the paper, briefly
38 Insanely
39 It may be delivered at a nightclub
40 Noted clown
41 Assocs.
42 Deejay Casey
43 Epitome of thinness
45 Pen name
46 Mama of pop music
47 Word in a Captain and Tennille title
51 Token room?
54 Drops the ball

55 Pie-mode link
56 Bird in a crazy simile
57 Hard-to-pronounce word
60 Vended
61 Jai ___
62 Famous Butler
63 Sanction
64 Icarus appendage
65 Lee and Teasdale

DOWN

1 Give a point to
2 Rock concert venue, sometimes
3 Plumber's concerns
4 Viper
5 Boards with ups and downs
6 "Dynasty" actress
7 Sheriff Taylor's boy
8 Mil. branch
9 Personal trainer's target
10 Jim-dandy
11 Vitamin additive, sometimes
12 Opener on Broadway?
13 Gift for a diva, perhaps
18 Great thing to be on
23 Royal symbol
25 Circus confection
26 They may be hard to swallow
28 Falsify, in a way
29 Aussie hoppers, briefly
30 It's a drag
31 Goblet feature
32 Ballplayer Ty

33 Shawm follower
34 Maugham's "___ of Lambeth"
35 Reiner and Perkins
38 Saskatchewan city
42 Mugs
44 Launch site
45 Duel personality?
47 Character in gangster film spoofs
48 Suburbanite, on some autumn days
49 Prince Valiant's wife
50 Some pastries
51 Furthermore
52 Fischer's castle
53 A caffeine source
54 McGregor of "Trainspotting"
58 He stung like a bee
59 "So, there you are!"

THE WORKS

By Alice Walker

ACROSS

1 Sound of an angry exit
5 Kosovo dweller, perhaps
9 Low area of land
14 Put something on board
15 Telltale sign
16 Calvin's pal Hobbes, e.g.
17 Dutch or convection follower
18 First of a famous sailing trio
19 Origins of a phoenix
20 Lock
23 Bakery offering
24 Famous invasion date
25 Some races
28 Unforeseen obstacle
29 Monkey's uncle?
32 Outlying community
33 Ill-gotten gain
34 Woeful expression
35 Stock
38 Some Wordsworth works
39 Top of the line
40 Alex Trebek, e.g.
41 Trophy locale, perhaps
42 Prove one can carry a tune
43 Become conscious
44 Place for a vault
45 Benediction closer
46 Barrel
53 Vena cava neighbor
54 Reap
55 Embryo of an invention
56 Bad gut feeling?
57 Parched

58 Seasonal tune
59 Data for salespeople
60 Dumas, ___
61 "What ___ can I say?"

DOWN

1 Hog filler
2 Molten spew
3 Arabian Sea gulf
4 Evelyn Waugh novel
5 Sub detectors
6 King's proclamation
7 "Oxford Blues" heroine
8 Subject of a trademark, perhaps
9 POW camp of WWII
10 Like cigarette smoke
11 Turkish honorific
12 Lascivious look
13 Formerly, once
21 Perchance
22 "Haste makes waste," e.g.
25 What greenskeepers do sometimes
26 Radiate, as charm
27 Unit of luminous flux
28 Musical genre
29 Woeful expression
30 Check list member?
31 Chief city of the Ruhr River valley
33 More than hard-of-hearing
34 Deep violet-red garnet
36 Bluffer's ploy

37 A flycatcher
42 Primitive weapons
43 What expiators make
44 Didn't dillydally
45 Month of showers
46 Road to Damascus figure, later
47 Play thing?
48 Whale of an attraction
49 An Indian may be wrapped in it
50 "American ___"
51 Wine vat waste
52 Institution founded in 1701

BATTY

By Carl Cranby

ACROSS

1 Moat menace, briefly
5 On or about
10 Place for change
14 Word with happy or eleventh
15 Make into law
16 Verb with down or out
17 Shop sign
19 Naysayer
20 Freshman on the bench
21 Cry from a nest over water
23 Brit. honor
24 It cannot be returned
25 Make coffee, in a way
26 "Kalifornia" star
28 Consent concern
31 Word with space or soap
34 Sweet-smelling necklace
35 Part of some film reviews
36 Loony
40 King of entertainment
41 Industrial container
42 Usher's post, often
43 French appellation
44 Mr. with the Mrs. and Mrs.
47 Kyrgyzstan range
48 Test req.
49 High-tech defense initials
52 "Little Women" author
55 On a tilt
57 Dear partner
58 Bizarre
60 Philosopher Immanuel
61 Kind of range

62 Need an ice bag, e.g.
63 Vicinity
64 Eyesores, really (Var.)
65 Unexpected slide

DOWN

1 It may be struck
2 Lounge lizards, e.g.
3 Trump
4 Some computer displays, briefly
5 Toyota model
6 Habituated
7 Unleash a diatribe
8 VI x L
9 Muscular
10 Best Actress, 1999
11 Make advances
12 Promising words?
13 Small combo
18 Mitchell clan
22 If it's a bust, it still qualifies as this
25 Landing on the water
26 Fiber source
27 Rio de la ___
28 Resigned remark
29 Kind of talk
30 Dueling sword
31 Middle East sultanate
32 ___ Alto, California
33 Dutch town or type of food
35 Marker
37 Certain United workers

1	2	3	4	■	5	6	7	8	9	■	10	11	12	13
14				■	15					■	16			
17			18							■	19			
20							■	21	22					
23			■	24			■	25				■	■	■
■	■	26				27				■	28	29	30	
31	32	33		■	■	34			■	35				
36				37	38				39					
40			■	41			■	42						
43			■	44			45	46		■	■	■	■	
■	■	47				■	48			■	49	50	51	
52	53	54			■	55			56					
57			■	58	59				■	60				
60			■	61				■	62					
63			■	64				■	65					

38 "The Gift of the ___"
39 Minor but aggravating problem
44 Meal known by its initials
45 Sleeveless coat
46 Furlong's 7,920
47 Carrier from the left ventricle
49 Cheese and crackers, e.g.

50 Jawaharlal Nehru University state
51 Twiddled one's thumbs
52 "Puppy Love" singer
53 TV producer Norman
54 Nursing home aid, perhaps
55 Uncertain
56 "When ___ a lad ..."
59 Temper tantrum

HEAD TO TOE

By Lynn Lempel

ACROSS

1 Hardly modern
6 Cartoon supply company
10 Edicts
14 D-Day beach
15 Manifesto writer
16 "Scram!"
17 CAP
19 Many a former Yugoslavian
20 Editor's override
21 Carbon-14 determination
22 Dolphins' domain
23 Neophyte
24 TEE
27 Hosp. staffers
29 Perseveres
30 Best supporting actress for "Girl, Interrupted"
33 Some push-ups
35 Top layer?
38 SHORTS
42 Asian holiday
43 Mouth-related
44 Bears Hall of Famer Mike
45 Raise
48 Immigrants' prep class, perhaps
49 SOCKS
53 Painter with a museum in St. Petersburg
57 "The Luck of Roaring Camp" writer
58 Nemo's harpoonist
59 It may come after life

60 Big name in 1970s gymnastics
61 SNEAKS
64 Roman poet
65 Massage aids
66 Place for outdoor dining, perhaps
67 Mr. America's pride, perhaps
68 Jubilation
69 Candid

DOWN

1 Awaken
2 Handed or headed start
3 Long candle
4 Pretentious speech
5 It may go for a dip in the ocean
6 South-of-the-border buddy
7 Caravan member
8 X-ray follow-up, perhaps
9 Phone no. addition
10 Help out
11 Low blow
12 The Velvet Fog
13 Film based on a Ferber novel
18 Falls behind
22 Common title
25 Thrash about
26 River under the Brooklyn Bridge
28 Aquarium implement
30 Type of stream
31 ___ Miss

32 Sluggish
33 Result of labor?
34 Color TV pioneer
36 "A mouse!"
37 Org. for U.S. cryptologists
39 Noted seamstress
40 They might be sq.
41 Tusked beast
46 Pieces of eight?
47 '50s campaign name
48 Vortex

49 Battle cry
50 Bisect
51 Approach to an article
52 Actress Witherspoon
54 Major blood supplier
55 "E pluribus unum," e.g.
56 Reassuring phrase
61 Gear tooth
62 Be indisposed
63 Sunscreen meas.

LAUNDRY DAY
By Alicia Sweet

ACROSS

1 Problems for parents
5 Slate backers
10 Like one defusing a bomb
14 Without help
15 Having to do with bees
16 Spanish jar
17 Prepare to orate
20 Some students, briefly
21 Esurient
22 Extract by force
23 Disembarrass
24 Without warranty
25 Layers
29 Muck
30 Second name in cosmetics
33 Circus Maximus, e.g.
34 Dry Mongolian expanse
35 Fictional plantation
36 Find trouble
39 British blue blood
40 Den din
41 Troy story
42 It's fit for a pig
43 It's grand link
44 Security clearance
45 Skirmish
46 It held two tablets
47 Didn't take any cards
49 Adolescent affliction
50 Snowmobile part
53 Simply give up
56 It's got ewe covered?
57 Lecture souvenirs
58 Have status
59 Likelihood ratio
60 Fescue, for one
61 Biblical patriarch

DOWN

1 Philosophical holdings
2 North African Muslim
3 "Not only that ..."
4 Ampersand follower, often
5 One view from the Baltic Sea
6 Plant louse
7 Trussed
8 Harbors
9 Kid's winter wear
10 What a rookie has to learn?
11 Church robes
12 Novelist's thread
13 Push to the limit
18 Kiltie's pattern
19 Drought-scourged
24 Shady spot
25 Thinkers full of wisdom
26 Unexpected pleasure
27 Give it a second shot
28 Indigo dye
29 Composer George M.
30 Bar-the-door gal
31 Regions
32 Feet are in them
34 Like hot fudge
35 Shower powder
37 Stepping on
38 Arch used in croquet

43 Forehead feature
44 "Gunsmoke" star
45 Type of gold
46 You may get these in the long run?
47 Rough finish?
48 Walked on

49 Lead-in to "boy" or "girl"
50 Cob or pen
51 Casino game
52 Varieties
53 Double standard?
54 Neither's partner
55 Rock hound's find, perhaps

TAKE NOTES

By Kane Wesley

ACROSS

1 Run out
6 Word with indigestion or test
10 Fly-swatter material
14 Lincoln's concern
15 Tube diameter
16 Dull discomfort
17 Winter dose, for some
19 Support for an old tire?
20 Kind of wind or treatment
21 Hilarious incident
22 Not just imagined
24 Dinner course
26 Unreliable witness
27 Something to do as you go?
28 Contemplated
32 Diamond feature
35 Undeniable
36 Kind of water
37 Word with history or hygiene
38 It may be in a skein
39 Without
40 Determination
41 Green-eyed monster
42 Noted book promoter
43 Berate
45 They grow when fertilized
46 Antonym for "out of"
47 Forebode
51 Burundi neighbor
54 Clairvoyant
55 Capacity-crowd letters
56 Bone-dry
57 Building toy unit

60 Constructed
61 Didn't swing at a pitch
62 Game site, perhaps
63 Sail support
64 Ocean prowlers, for short
65 Some spreads

DOWN

1 Clear
2 Arboreal lizard
3 They might be popped
4 Landscaper's need, sometimes
5 Supplicate
6 Trappist head
7 Revolver inventor
8 Vexation
9 Political prisoner, e.g.
10 It's usually covered in the bedroom
11 Linen hue
12 Big place in New York
13 It might be said to a dog
18 Subject to a draft
23 Scoundrel
25 Excellent speaker
26 Wretchedly bad
28 Verify
29 Safari sound
30 A first name on "The Simpsons"
31 100-yard contest
32 It may get by on chicken feed
33 Operatic highlight
34 Tranquil

35 Masked man's companion
38 Patterns of experience, in psychology
42 Cover some of the same territory
44 Frequent joiner
45 Classic snack
47 Quick kisses
48 Sea interrupter
49 Witchlike woman
50 Attire at some fraternity blasts
51 Some St. Louis athletes
52 Shrink trailer
53 Leontyne Price role
54 Stuffed shirt
58 Letters from a debtor?
59 Firearms org.

GOING STAG

By George Keller

ACROSS

1 A Day in Hollywood
6 French cleric
10 E-mail that's likely to be deleted
14 Rudimentary seed
15 Act of faith?
16 Sierra Maestra country
17 Jack
20 Proofreaders' oversights
21 Gung ho
22 Latakia's land
25 Common fraction
26 Tennyson poem
30 Tiny amount of progress
32 Deluge
35 Beat to the tape
41 Bill
43 Value highly
44 Tab picker-uppers
45 Hodgepodge
47 Plaudits of a sort
48 Drive back
53 Jousting weapon
56 Strange things
58 Dust jacket comments, e.g.
63 Bob
66 "Or ___!"
67 Relative affluence
68 Place for a sacred cow?
69 Casting requirement
70 Rockefeller company
71 Downright unpleasant

DOWN

1 Went to the bottom
2 Of higher rank than
3 German industrial region
4 Hipbones
5 Breakaway groups
6 Lager kin
7 Letter-perfect contest?
8 "The Human Comedy" author
9 Pointless weapon
10 Assayer's tool
11 Produce, as a show
12 Give or take
13 Waterlogged soil
18 Install, as a carpet
19 Cauldron, e.g.
23 Customary observance
24 Subject of the first law of motion
26 Chuck-a-luck equipment
27 Difficult task
28 Result of a lack of practice, metaphorically
29 It could precede a good deal
31 Get an edge
33 It may look for a buck
34 Snowballs, sometimes
36 Inst. founded by Jefferson
37 Baum canine
38 Capital of Cambodia?
39 It could be a lot or a plot
40 Monstrous lake
42 Something forged
46 "Camels" of the Andes

48 Direct elsewhere
49 Send to Siberia, e.g.
50 Western group
51 Ricky's landlady
52 Putting concern
54 Major broadcaster
55 Like Santa's helpers

57 Native American of the North
59 Human bone
60 Curtain inserts
61 Fish or cut this
62 Order to a dog
64 Biblical transport
65 "The Matrix" hero

PASTORAL VISTA

By Kelly Johnson

ACROSS
1 Home run hitter's gait
5 It's full of roots
10 Film terrier
14 Mister, abroad
15 Verboten
16 Impediment to smooth sailing
17 "Nay!" sayer
18 Town in Maine
19 Deal with it
20 Tree in need of comfort?
23 Silly Putty container
24 Opposite of paleo
25 "This is only ___"
28 Distributed the cards
30 Alluring skirt feature
33 Syndicate head
34 Formal speech
37 Reject one's betrothed
38 Celebratory lifting device?
41 Growth period
42 Sharply reduced, as a price
43 Mannequin part
44 Kind of loaf
45 Knock over a joint
49 Fred's sister and dance partner
51 Shoe designation for spindly feet
53 Baden-Baden or Aix-les-bains, e.g.
54 Stream of run-on sentences?
59 Roentgen discovery
61 Luckless fellow

62 Certain woodwind
63 Facilitate
64 State one's case
65 Indonesian island
66 Some have white tails
67 Davis of "Death on the Nile"
68 Prefix for while

DOWN
1 Prepared for cooking, in away
2 Not do as promised
3 Former president of Nicaragua
4 Stumble
5 Biblical weapon
6 Loadmaster's concern
7 Take ___ (acknowledge applause)
8 Burt's ex
9 Merge resources
10 Fancy tie
11 Stranded, in a way
12 Water outlet
13 Topic of many a lie
21 Emcee's job
22 Back muscle, to a bodybuilder
26 Cobbler's concern
27 Smithereens maker
29 Impend
30 Egyptian peninsula
31 Fireplace fodder
32 Type of worm
35 Chevet

36 Cash drawer
37 An overworked horse
38 Solemn promise
39 Runner's goal in baseball
40 Addict's program
41 Bleating sound
44 Rookie socialite
46 Line on the weather report
47 Thread holders
48 Start of an Eagles hit title

50 Wedding cake feature
51 Concerning
52 Correspond, grammatically
55 Film monster of 1958 and 1988
56 Slow running pace
57 Start of a guess
58 Garb for the bench
59 Crossed out
60 "Norma ___" (Sally Field film)

TRAVEL IN STYLE
By Lynn Lempel

ACROSS
1 Weight-training unit
4 Prevailed
7 Contest with boxers
14 Former
16 Gourmet
17 Melanesia locale
18 Picked apart
19 Preview of a sort
21 Prior to, to Prior
22 Word with after or through
23 Something for the poor
27 Odometer button
30 Hunk
34 Fluid-level reading, sometimes
36 "From Here to Eternity" setting
37 African antelope
38 Outstanding athlete
42 Reply
44 "To Kill a Mockingbird" character
45 Apple frequency?
47 Prefix for giving or taking
48 Printer type
51 Eyelashes
55 Olympian's weapon
56 Caddy's holding
58 Hall of Famer Mel
59 Slugger's guru
65 Herbaceous ornamental
68 Cover a point?
69 AC/DC converter
70 Like some clay pots
71 Stay alive
72 Rapid transit?
73 Snaky shape

DOWN
1 Boarder
2 Curtain call
3 Annoyances
4 Candlelight dinner accompaniment, perhaps
5 Skips
6 Approached
7 Ricky's portrayer
8 Birthstone after sapphire
9 Springiness
10 Deified beetle
11 Embrace
12 Rock deposit
13 Espoused
15 Asian language family
20 Saab model
24 Apple's apple, e.g.
25 Education reformer Horace
26 Wall support
28 Woods rival
29 Add up
31 Sound sense
32 Attention-seeking utterance
33 Some downloads
35 Use hip boots, e.g.
38 French priest's title
39 Half-mask
40 Occipital ___
41 Rule over India

43 Chi-omega connection
46 Bigfoot's cousin
49 Dances to jazz music, in a way
50 Grammar topics
52 Detest
53 Yens
54 Acropolis locale
57 Muslim titles (Var.)

60 Not in favor of
61 Alliances
62 Pastry offering
63 "Dead ___" (Francis book)
64 Stable morsel
65 ___-relief sculpture
66 Com alternative
67 Chatter

MOVE TO THE BEAT
By Wesley Kane

ACROSS

1 Epistle writer
5 Temple's first husband
9 Bar fare
14 One-time Delhi queen
15 Prefix meaning "minute"
16 Beethoven dedicatee
17 Garden bloom
18 Film villain
19 Invoice word
20 Beat
23 Barking mammal
24 Food for a flicker
25 Woodstock gear
28 Buttercup relative
31 Cain raiser
34 Henhouse perch
36 .0000001 joule
37 Overlook
38 Beat
42 Glimpse
43 Tempest in a teapot
44 Slake
45 A Partridge portrayer
46 Marked for life
49 Allen wrench shape
50 Play parent for a night
51 Essayist's alias
53 Beat
60 Type of system or badge
61 Fiesta fare, perhaps
62 Clue weapon
63 Griffin part
64 Kitten's plaything

65 "The Camp Meeting" composer
66 Garson of "Madame Curie"
67 One of a matched set
68 Piggy-bank deposit

DOWN

1 Stuck-up one
2 Bern is on it
3 Word with military or heating
4 Shopping memos
5 Cuzco native
6 Distort, in a way
7 Stuart queen
8 Dig like a pig
9 Completely calm
10 Wide-eyed
11 Prom night wheels, briefly
12 "Clueless" exclamation
13 NYPD title
21 Tract of wasteland
22 Latin dance
25 Dangerous go-with
26 Large northern deer
27 Type of seed
29 Produce item
30 Precious metal, in Madrid
31 Writer Zola
32 Like some statistics or organs
33 Gas for Merman?
35 Place for pen pals?
37 Barn bird
39 Inheritance of the meek

40 Pharmaceuticals overseer,
   for short
41 Woody Allen's "___ Days"
46 Kind of pill
47 Winter aid for windshields
48 Nudges, in a way
50 Subway feature
52 Savory jelly

53 Juicy fruit
54 Compulsion
55 Imprint
56 Headless cabbage
57 One place to find your honey
58 Lead the bidding
59 Arboreal abode
60 "Little Women" woman

CREEPED OUT

By Carl Cranby

ACROSS

1 Divulge a secret
5 Sainted mother of Constantine
11 Roll of dough?
14 Mythical mischief-maker
15 Not involving questions of right or wrong
16 Cheer for a toreador
17 Sheep genus
18 Picture book?
19 Pool table success
20 Creepy crawler
22 Card game for a sot?
24 Thorny bunch
25 Singer Ives
26 Stonecutter
29 Some medical buildings
32 Stamp-making org.
33 Sharp emotional attacks
36 Pulitzer-winning Akins
37 Enjoy Aspen, perhaps
38 Pythagorean proposition
39 Legal org.
40 Jack and Bobby's brother
41 Spoke from the soapbox
42 Limo destination, sometimes
43 Knitted garment
45 In a wild and crazy way
46 Ceremony
47 Some hotel amenities
50 "Filthy" money
52 Creepy creature
56 Commit a faux pas, perhaps
57 Bookworm

59 Dashing style
60 Nabokov novel
61 Elegant fur
62 Apartment, e.g.
63 Pencil stump, e.g.
64 Treats a broken bone
65 Rajah's mate

DOWN

1 Group voting the same way
2 All-conquering thing
3 Related (to)
4 Informal cafes
5 Hinged fasteners
6 Host a show
7 Noblemen
8 Toledo's body of water
9 Preschooler's dread
10 Selflessness
11 Creepy crawler
12 Certain astringent
13 Contradict
21 Electron-deficient atom, perhaps
23 Keats praised one
25 Run, as ink
26 Essential items
27 Lopsided
28 Creepy sidler
29 Heart
30 Computer-programming language
31 Disreputable
33 Number of storied bears

34 Listen and pay attention
35 Decay
38 One with an unsteady gait
42 French chemist and vaccine developer
44 Radial fill
45 Chess units
47 Hawkins of Dogpatch
48 Contraction between looks and everything

49 Kramden's collections
50 Supermarket meat label, perhaps
51 Language of Pakistan
52 Scottish caps
53 Arm bone
54 Past participle of lie
55 Prefix for bodies
58 Before, in poesy

GOING TO COURT
By Thomas Hollingsworth

ACROSS

1 Flat-topped elevation
5 Gifts in a Christmas carol
10 Savoir-faire
14 Farm team
15 Creed component
16 Jai ___
17 Court
20 Street in a horror film
21 Mother of Helen of Troy
22 Genetic duplicates
23 Like a mansion
25 It requires 32 cards
26 Word in the MGM motto
27 The Hatfields, e.g.
28 "What ___, chopped liver?"
31 Low-tech calculators
34 Honey of a wine
35 Type of man or horse
36 Court
39 "I smell ___!"
40 Traditional story
41 One-time rulers
42 Tach reading
43 Jacuzzi tubs, e.g.
44 Romanian money
45 Like the Grinch
46 Legendary siren
50 "Eat crow" and "talk turkey"
53 One and only
54 UK reference book
55 Court
58 Author Wiesel
59 Summon up

60 Where most people are
61 Fly catcher
62 Used a needle
63 Hair salons stock them

DOWN

1 Wears a long face
2 Glorify
3 Bart Simpson's aunt
4 Collected sayings, e.g.
5 Braces against
6 Like an untended garden
7 She taught in Siam
8 Place to surf without a board
9 One place for prisoners
10 Divination deck
11 King of the entertainment field
12 Pet store purchase, perhaps
13 Many are purchased in June
18 Parson, e.g.
19 ___ Bator, Mongolian capital
24 Implied
25 Cut with sweeping strokes
27 Occupiers of Britain and
   Spain in pre-Roman times
28 Diva's showcase
29 Certain North African Muslim
30 Rural lodges
31 Cracked a bit
32 After-dinner faux pas
33 First of all?
34 Mexican native, perhaps
35 Come forth
37 Dead ends

38 Sound system
43 Automatic starter?
44 Dawdled
45 Haystacks painter
46 "The Gauntlet" actress, 1977
47 Wretchedly bad
48 Like a Stephen King story
49 Brainstorm results, sometimes
50 News dispatch
51 Kind of loaf
52 "What's ___ for me?"
53 Winter fall
56 Nervous time, maybe
57 Sorrowful

BRUSH ASIDE

By Alicia Sweet

ACROSS

1 Guy in a sty
5 Divide
9 In process
14 "... ___ to leap tall buildings ..."
15 Perched on
16 Stars with fluctuating brightness
17 1969 music event
19 Persona non ___
20 Reason to serve again
21 11th U.S. president
22 Vacillate
23 One way to keep a boat afloat
24 Some cruise ship employees
25 Water droplets aloft
28 Deserving the booby prize
29 Come to an end, like a subscription
30 Kind of sheet used in class
31 Rope material
35 Beehive State
36 "If I do ___ myself ..."
37 Stereotypical name for a sci-fi lab assistant
38 Time unit at sea
39 Whimper
40 Pancakes and sour cream
41 More than punctual
43 Aromatic ointment
44 Publicly expressed honors
47 Low man in the choir

48 Point on an orbit
49 Word with star or ranger
50 Crazy way to go
53 Summer TV fare
54 Alex Raymond's cartoon character
56 Put at bay
57 City on the Oka, near Moscow
58 Island east of Java
59 Spicy sauce
60 Roberts' co-star, twice
61 Rabbit of fiction

DOWN

1 Cry one's eyes out
2 The duck in "Peter and the Wolf"
3 What little things mean?
4 Valentine's Day's signature color
5 Regional dialect
6 Ringlike coral island
7 Word with salt or garden
8 Toll hwy.
9 Brings to the boiling point
10 Queens tennis community
11 Not perfectly round
12 Tom Mix film, e.g.
13 Winter Palace residents
18 Digging tool
22 Option on some sporty cars
23 One goes through these to get to the majors

24 Model's asset
25 Word with night or bridge
26 Emu's tail?
27 Certain gemstone
28 With a touch of irony, often
30 Hats from nets
32 Sponsorship (Var.)
33 Leonardo's subject
34 Strait-laced
36 Binge
40 Swiss city on the Rhine
42 Plan of action

43 Rigid bracelet
44 Some deer
45 "Turandot," for one
46 Edible mushroom
47 Silly blunder
49 Work as a barker, e.g.
50 Partially open
51 Carpet component
52 Middle Eastern prince
54 Nudge, as the memory
55 Flow partner

SPOOKED!

By Alice Walker

ACROSS

1 Mecca trek (Var.)
5 Riding costume
10 Lop the crop, e.g.
14 Distant leader
15 Squash variety
16 Black-and-white creature
17 Hardly a Westminster contender
18 It may unfold around a campfire
20 International accord, e.g.
21 Solitaire, e.g.
22 Gardens amidst the sands
23 Subject for Dante
25 Trail marker
28 Items in a record
31 Branch of mathematics
35 Code name?
36 Unskilled person
38 Stalactite former
39 Poem written to be sung, perhaps
40 Multiplex multitude
43 Be choosy?
44 Lacrimal droplet
46 Wild ones are sown
47 Run ___ (get into trouble)
49 Where a river meets the sea
51 Deficient in amount or quality
53 Full of chutzpah
55 Goes in haste
56 Unemotional
59 Start of Cain's query
61 It's sometimes made in the dark
64 Astringent alcoholic solution
67 Fork point
68 Choir voice
69 Perfect in all ways
70 Treads the boards
71 Broadway luminary?
72 Far from tanned
73 Helicopter runners

DOWN

1 Sackcloth material
2 Light blue-green
3 It may require separate checks
4 Nerves
5 A way to barter
6 Word with ear or back
7 Certain mike supports
8 It has many schedules
9 It can be a real blast
10 Did a tire-maintenance job
11 Greek god of love
12 Suburban plot, maybe
13 Remunerates
19 Dance partner?
24 Creates fiction
26 Loving touch
27 North Carolina university
28 Play to the back row
29 Protuberances
30 Moves away from the flock
32 Witch craft?
33 Tear to shreds

34 With competence
37 To date
41 J.C. Dithers' wife in "Blondie"
42 Indian wraparound
45 Caesar crossed it
48 Festive celebrations
50 Foot curve
52 Uncomfortably cool
54 Rags an initiate

56 Famous lake
57 Kind of floor
58 Palindromic emperor
60 Potatoes partner
62 Not in favor of
63 Harry Truman's wife
65 Word with hop or joint
66 Nabokov novel

WINDOW DISPLAY

By Elizabeth C. Gorski

ACROSS

1 Time to get back to work, perhaps
6 Waitress with Sam and Coach
11 Gasps of delight
14 Ill-fated vessel Andrea ___
15 Crunchy snacks
16 Like sashimi
17 Elizabeth's love
18 Nuts and bolts
19 Before, in poems
20 Navy, for one
22 Mary Todd's love
23 Wimbledon unit
24 It may be cast
25 Alarm or art add-on
26 Space-saving bed
27 Wood tool
28 City on the Allegheny
30 Snooze stentoriously
32 Jazz violinist Jean-___ Ponty
33 Fractional monetary unit of Japan
35 Major trading center of Arabia
36 Play before the play
40 Words of alarm
41 Pilot's heading, perhaps
42 Acapulco article
43 City north of Dallas
45 Sound at an NBA game
47 Income provided by the U.S. govt.
50 Kind of rope or truck
51 Cole who was "King"
53 PBS benefactor
54 Shade at the beach?
55 Farsighted investment, briefly
56 Cul-de-sacs, basically
59 Russian space station
60 '50s presidential hopeful Stevenson
61 Likely to creep one out
62 Get ___ for effort
63 Soothing ointment
64 Abbreviated vacation goal, sometimes
65 "___ Miserables"
66 Slalom curves
67 Bamboo unit

DOWN

1 "Battleship Potemkin" setting
2 Snacked
3 Artificial
4 With different colored patches
5 Like some credit cards
6 Energizer for some
7 Certain bazaargoer
8 Couch potato's site, perhaps
9 Yoga position
10 Pieces of property, e.g.
11 Certain numerical prefix
12 One hiding fugitives, e.g.
13 Make less bitter, in a way
21 Tin Man's accessory
29 Good ___ (repaired)
31 Rocket launcher

32 Author Hubbard
34 Motion of the ocean result, sometimes
36 Water purifier
37 One way to be caught
38 Imparts
39 Asthmatics' needs, sometimes
40 Best

44 Where leadoff hitters want to be
46 West ___ (Jamaica's home)
47 Jelly used for fuel
48 Officially leave bachelorhood
49 Sunday newspaper feature
52 Father-and-son actors
57 Main cathedral area
58 Jacob's wife

NOT SO FAST

By George Wesley

ACROSS

1 Acct. ledger entries
5 What little things mean?
9 American Revolution supporters
14 What an out-turned palm may mean
15 Turpentine source
16 Hellish place
17 Eye lasciviously
18 Become wearisome
19 Von Bulow portrayer
20 Slowly but surely
23 Tamperer hamperer
24 Turn right
25 Rhea's Roman counterpart
28 In a heads-up manner
31 On the warpath
34 Rolls out the red carpet for
36 Queenside castle, in chess notation
37 Bulletin-board posting, perhaps
38 How some build
42 Unbleached muslin shade
43 Vietnam annex?
44 Uncaged
45 White alternative
46 Plant's principal feeder
49 Ron who hit 316 home runs
50 Bump hard
51 Like a blue moon
53 How a baby progresses?
60 Not quite right

61 Guitar forerunner
62 Word with happy or eleventh
63 Gumption
64 Roman god of love
65 Bluesy James
66 Show subservience, in a way
67 Science fiction site
68 Willard's cohorts

DOWN

1 Gone wrong?
2 "The Gift of the ___"
3 Begin to fall
4 Manuscript annotations, perhaps
5 Legal tactic
6 Responsible
7 One partner
8 Show partner
9 Beaver's friend
10 "The Luck of Roaring Camp" writer
11 Fan mail recipient
12 Something from a parent
13 Sound of air escaping
21 Lowest in importance
22 Hemispherical home
25 Buyer's proposal
26 Shelley's first name
27 Buyer be where?
29 Runner Bannister
30 Rocky pinnacle
31 A Bordeaux wine
32 Be a class clown

33 Bashful companion?
35 Grounded bird
37 Phone-dial trio
39 Courage
40 More than mere intuition
41 Sound beginning?
46 Graduation cap part
47 Demosthenes, for one
48 Formula Westerns
50 He marched with Martin

52 Old-time anesthetic
53 Augury
54 Largest digit
55 Son of Shem
56 Mountain lion
57 Scintilla
58 Pound inmate, often
59 Stats for pitchers
60 Interpellate

PUFF THE MAGIC DRAGON

By Lane Gutz

ACROSS

1 Pursuits of good reporters
6 About 15 klicks northeast of Amsterdam
10 Hot to trot
14 Eyelet insert
15 Upper part of a glacier
16 Stopping point?
17 Some social gatherings
19 Italian stringed instrument
20 Billy Shears in a Beatles movie
22 Small amount of solid food
24 Magical
25 One-eighty
26 Word with raid or strike
27 Word from a giant
28 Giants legend Mel
30 Greek letter
31 Having a missing part
33 One way to set a clock
35 One-time presidential hopeful
38 Iris containers
39 Philadelphia university
42 Homer's exclamation
45 Words that end an engagement
46 One of Jacob's sons
47 Feel sickly
48 Many Middle Easterners
50 ___ de Triomphe
51 A WMD
52 Follower of Jesus
56 Jazz vocal form

57 Unsuitable for surgery
60 "What ___ can go wrong?"
61 Truth alternative
62 "... bombs bursting ___"
63 Not so much!
64 They get fleeced
65 Revenge-seekers of film

DOWN

1 Some chew it
2 Fatigue factor
3 Pretentious prose
4 Flap-door shelter
5 Something for the record books, briefly
6 Course for a gourmet
7 More than lionize
8 State with certainty
9 It's less extensive than a plateau
10 Make it work
11 Vice antithesis
12 Bring in from abroad
13 Actress Durbin
18 Like some used ink cartridges
21 It changes genes
22 Scrooge exclamation
23 Sundial hour
27 Early 20th-century French art style
28 Sound of surprise
29 Squid's feeler
32 Greek letter
33 Hinny's kin

34 Hoover, for one
36 Eastern belief
37 The longest key
40 Word with women's or ad
41 Common street name
42 Young maiden
43 Delphi prophet
44 Bother blatantly
46 They can be pulled

49 Computer memory units
50 Absolutely love
51 Absolutely ridiculous
53 Office assistant
54 Emulate a mouse
55 "___ Brockovich"
58 In keeper?
59 Sounds of hesitation

DOESN'T ADD UP

By Kacie Eller

ACROSS

1 First part of a Florida city
5 First place of habitation
9 Valerie Harper series
14 ___ elephant (part of a tot's lesson)
15 Western postwar alliance
16 Invisible emanations
17 Start of a quip
20 Solder or soldier material
21 Riles
22 Lose
23 Word with pick or pack
24 Right-turn command
25 Directions word
26 Quip (Part 2)
33 Shaker or Bkln.
34 Indeterminate number
35 Taj Mahal's locale
36 Husbands and wives
39 Steak go-with
40 Nebraska natives
41 Over again
42 Punching tool
43 Hospital lines
44 Quip (Part 3)
50 Shrewdly tricky
51 "___ So Fine" (The Chiffons)
52 Hagen of Broadway
53 Sightlessness
57 "Gone With the Wind" estate
58 Fiddle stick?
59 End of the quip
62 Having to do with bees

63 Huck's transport
64 Vogue competitor
65 Takes ten
66 Gaelic tongue
67 Welfare state?

DOWN

1 Michael Jackson hit
2 Kind of pool or park
3 Optometrist's concern
4 Indonesian islands
5 Menu heading
6 Less lit
7 Pilots' approximations, briefly
8 "Ripley's Believe It or ___!"
9 Michelin introduced it in 1946
10 Close-mouthed singing
11 Like some vaccines
12 Kind of bank or base
13 Like a fireplace floor
18 Something to take in
19 Post of propriety
25 Transport for Tarzan
27 Like caramel
28 Half of a Washington city
29 Unkind nickname for a corpulent man
30 Teamwork spoiler
31 Poet's preposition
32 ___ Palmas
36 Longtime Chinese leader
37 Raggedy doll
38 Business-card abbr.

39 Off-kilter
40 Egg container
42 One of the black keys
43 Sound like a broken record
45 People with the most people
46 Shucks
47 Marriageable
48 Actor Peter of "The Lion in Winter"

49 Kowtowed
53 Slightly open
54 Casual dissent
55 Some sashes
56 Exam for jrs.
57 Peter the Great, e.g.
60 Vexation
61 Half a score

MAKE UP YOUR MIND

By Sarah Keller

ACROSS
1 Boatyard
6 Beijing housemaid
10 Argue back and forth
14 At a good clip, poetically
15 Modify
16 Whine and whimper
17 Muscular strength
18 Pro
20 C'___ la vie
21 If this fits, wear it!
23 Fruit type high in vitamin C
24 Dangerous kind of wedding?
26 One in Bonn
27 ___ Tin Tin
28 Shaken up
33 Like crashing waves
36 Buzzing pest
37 Verdi princess
38 Neutral place to be
41 Early Ron Howard role
42 Fonda title role
43 Historic Alabama march site
44 Produced a likeness of
46 Solfeggio syllable
47 Apple pie partner?
48 Cricket's cousin
52 Tough call for a bettor
56 It's built on
57 Investment vehicle, for short
58 Against
60 Hold, as the attention
62 Dance with Virginia?
63 Refreshing way to start?

64 Without substance
65 On a single occasion
66 Sha ___ (doo-wop group)
67 Chaplin props

DOWN
1 They're sometimes loaded
2 Prone to imitation
3 ___ Domingo
4 Bar basic
5 Certain paper deliverer
6 Word on an envelope from
   abroad, perhaps
7 Equine feature
8 Sandy's sound
9 Zircon variety
10 Dick's dog
11 Contented sound
12 Felipe or Moises of baseball
13 KO callers
19 It's creepy
22 Ostrogoth's foe
25 Gave and got
26 On the maternal side
28 Like an expired parking meter
29 Hardly ever
30 Bowed musical instrument
31 Mild, yellow Dutch cheese
32 Arp's art
33 Roman god of love
34 Ready on the vine
35 Father of Thor
36 Artificially created human, in
   Jewish folklore

39 Frenchman or Swede, e.g.
40 Not for the masses
45 Grounded Australian birds
46 Was not off one's rocker?
48 Plains Native American
49 Backless sofa
50 Dunne of "I Remember Mama"
51 For marriages, they're set
52 Corrida participant
53 Frank
54 It's sometimes built on
55 Lone fish?
56 British weapon
59 Carrier of genetic info
61 Words with nutshell

ALL THE RIGHT ANGLES

By James E. Buell

ACROSS

1 Meted out
6 One-time Nintendo rival
10 Expensive car trips?
14 Open central courts
15 Cast forth
16 "Dies ___"
17 Puzzle fad
19 One-time Israeli prime minister
20 Old Tokyo
21 End to all you can
22 Words with "more than you can chew"
24 Address of St. Patrick's Cathedral?
26 Frigid and Torrid, e.g.
27 Prohibit legally
29 Former Russian sovereigns
33 Wheat husk
36 Have as a subsidiary
37 Blockbuster's offspring
38 Kind of trap
39 Musical repeat sign
41 Take apart
42 A to A, e.g.
44 Word with wax or phone
45 Resting on
46 Camp meal, perhaps
47 You'll gain leverage with this
49 "Flashdance" star
51 Compensates for a loss
55 It borders Uzbekistan
58 School liaison org.
59 Swiss canton
60 Mexican capital
61 Concertina
64 Like some proportions
65 Drum out
66 "The Waste Land" penner
67 Charge too much
68 They may be split or sweet
69 Melodramatic

DOWN

1 Shows courage
2 Certain musical composition
3 Shade-creating structure
4 XIII x IV
5 Tackle
6 Splinter group
7 It has wings but cannot fly
8 Tailless primate
9 Had a traditional dinner
10 Where the ball is dropped
11 Twistable cookie
12 Very thin model, e.g.
13 Feudal peasant
18 Warwick needed directions here
23 French noggin
25 Writer's dread
26 Witty, pointed retorts
28 Have unpaid bills
30 Polly, to Tom Sawyer
31 Decorate anew
32 Zero-star meal, maybe
33 Voting coalition
34 Calorie-laden

35 Lock opener?
37 Material that's absorbed
40 Thumbs-down vote
43 Strives for victory
47 Commemorative wall-hanging
48 Floors
50 Fabulist of yore
52 Ancient Nile Valley kingdom
53 Lose tautness

54 Mile-a-minute speed
55 Heston's captors, in film
56 Vehicle at an auction, perhaps
57 Polo field?
58 They may lie around the house
62 Where many things are made
63 Lynne's band, familiarly

FILMING GEOMETRY

By Isaiah Burke

ACROSS

1 ___-Am (Dr. Seuss character)
5 Isn't passive
9 Genesis
14 Arabian Sea gulf
15 More than interested in someone's business
16 Lake near Carson City
17 Gang territory
18 Gouda cousin
19 Risible beast
20 Transplanted Acropolis sculptures
23 Acoustic term
24 Driller's quest, often
25 Old French coin
28 Memory lapses
32 Follower of Christ?
35 One with a sought-after list
36 The "O" in magazines
37 Chorus member
39 The eyes have it
42 Race terminus
43 Metamorphic stage
45 Not yet a marquis
47 Space abode, once
48 Test of public opinion
52 Electrical measure, for short
53 Long-bodied fish
54 Seizes without authority
58 Fun for the rescue squad
61 Doughboy's weapon
64 Pusher's bane
65 Revelation

66 Fervor
67 Sedan sweetie
68 The good earth?
69 Dilapidated cars
70 Anatomical pouches
71 Budget meeting?

DOWN

1 Surfeits
2 One never seen in "Peanuts"
3 Enter traffic
4 Weak and feeble
5 Buttercup relatives
6 Closing musical passage
7 Despotic ruler
8 Something standing for something else
9 Shakespeare character
10 Side in a vote
11 "Murder, ___ Wrote"
12 Long geological time period
13 Genteel affair
21 Prerequisite
22 Ad add-on
25 Vamoose
26 Giraffe's striped kin
27 One who walks down the aisle?
29 ___ chi
30 Spiritual being
31 Make up your mind
32 Sicily's neighbor
33 Car protector
34 Las Vegas area

38 Eggs, in science
40 Twain portrayer Holbrook
41 Beats decisively
44 Mediterranean capital
46 Basis for a claim
49 Exclude
50 Sports venues
51 Suitable for marriage
55 Dangerous emission

56 State "Not guilty," e.g.
57 Gives a very poor review to
58 Broadway bomb
59 "___ Told Me (Not to Come)"
60 Idle from Monty Python
61 Jock support?
62 Wrath
63 U.S. health watchdog

SELF-IMPROVEMENT VOWS

By George Keller

ACROSS

1 Egyptian cobras
5 Fashionable
9 San Antonio tourist stop
14 Lacey on "Cagney & Lacey"
15 Word with mark or slinger
16 Character assassination
17 ___ Bator (capital of Mongolia)
18 Spicy Spanish stew
19 Unsavory character
20 I vow to …
23 Jerry's cartoon foe
24 Discovery at Sutter's Mill
25 Slip up
26 Computer of film
28 Wolf's warning
30 Vampire slayer
32 Of a previous time
33 Sundial numeral
35 Barbarian
36 Emulating a sleepyhead
37 I vow to …
42 What a siren does
43 It's for the course?
44 Keen longing
45 Canton of William Tell
46 Wearing less
48 Type of fire
52 Clansman's topper
53 Mountain climber's challenge
54 Mentally quick
56 What wasting food is, according to moms

57 I vow to …
61 It's full of holes
62 Bear of a constellation
63 Part of a futhark
64 Facilitator
65 Fish feature
66 Italian volcano
67 A password provides it
68 "… not always what they ___"
69 Beyond recharging

DOWN

1 Grown people
2 Miss Kitty's place of employment
3 Type of TV
4 Year's last word
5 Mormon Tabernacle, for one
6 Bisects
7 Man in the Irish Sea?
8 Evian toppers
9 Appeal
10 Zodiac animal
11 One of the United Arab Emirates
12 Communiques
13 Toreador's acclaim
21 Sheet of print
22 Island group off Scotland
27 Mother of mine?
29 Become prominent
31 Consoling word
34 Pierce with a point

36 Adolescent's bane
37 Flood, as a market
38 Pertaining to both sides of the Urals
39 Most toned
40 Parental purchase for a rock concert?
41 Right-hand page
46 Torte vendor
47 Grapple, to Li'l Abner

49 Very perceptive
50 Reddish-brown pigment, when burnt
51 Group of nine
55 One of a biblical 150
58 End of a walkie-talkie transmission
59 Great Lakes name
60 Ginger's partner
61 "Didn't I tell you?"

A FORTUNATE PUZZLE

By Thomas Hollingsworth

ACROSS

1 Jeanne d'Arc's title (Abbr.)
4 Lightweight hat
10 Bausch's partner
14 ___ in Charles
15 Excessively ornamented
16 Revered one
17 Flop opposite
18 No real consolation
20 Nails down just right
22 Type of guide
23 Chancel
24 Biblical dead place
26 A wife of Charlie Chaplin
28 Holiday helper
30 Bad luck
33 Move emotionally
34 Samples
35 Pluck eyebrow hairs, e.g.
37 Proof of ownership
40 Engaged in repartee
41 Cuban ballerina Alicia
42 Harbor of Hawaii
43 Clothing store department
44 West Coast football pro
49 Desktop devices
50 Type of American
51 Make a sound in the night?
52 "Who Framed Roger Rabbit" character
54 "Wasn't me!"
57 Feta source
58 Assume responsibility in another's absence

61 "Spring ahead" letters
62 Words in a popular palindrome
63 Mount Hood locale
64 Count Tolstoy
65 To be, in old Rome
66 Tough boss to work for
67 Directional suffix

DOWN

1 A division into factions
2 Chinese exercises
3 Lauder and Chandler
4 Gomer Pyle's rank
5 Oodles
6 ___ contendere
7 Burdensome
8 One millionth of a meter
9 Ruckus
10 Jacket opener?
11 Dashboard display
12 Emulate Aesop
13 Eatery order, perhaps
19 Postgrad deg.
21 Lessens in force
25 Large-eyed primate
27 Take-home amount
29 Mister Rogers
31 Swindle
32 Vietnamese New Year
33 "The Twilight Zone" creator
36 Admonishes
37 Use it to change levels
38 Qualified voters

1	2	3		4	5	6	7	8	9		10	11	12	13
14				15							16			
17				18						19				
20			21		22					23				
24				25			26		27			28		29
30					31	32					33			
			34						35	36				
37	38	39						40						
41							42							
43					44	45					46	47	48
49				50						51				
	52		53			54		55	56		57			
58					59					60		61		
62					63							64		
65					66							67		

39 Allays sorrow
40 Part of a musical gig
42 Mistake-catcher
45 Mean as a snake
46 Ribbon of pasta
47 It clears the boards
48 Gymnast Mary Lou

50 Picnic intruder
53 "Garfield" dog
55 Roman raiment
56 Curling tool
58 Half a bray
59 Stolen
60 Blaster's need

IT'S ON YOUR SIDE

By Alicia Sweet

ACROSS

1 Help out in a scam
5 Like some textbooks
9 Once and again
14 Nominate
15 Move toward
16 Use a stationary bike
17 Start of a timely definition
20 Underhanded
21 Vast South American region
22 Mantel piece, perhaps
23 British bombshell Diana
24 Slugging stat
26 Have respect for
29 Causation study
34 Low dam
35 Switch words?
36 Stubbed item
37 Timely definition (Part 2)
41 Pythagorean P
42 Wayne Gretzky, until 1988
43 Take it on the chin
44 Tarnish
46 Selected
48 Shelley praise
49 Sticky stuff
50 Brit's baby carriage
53 Less calm
56 Fill in
59 End of the definition
62 Mississippi quartet
63 Aqua or cosmo trailer
64 Low tract
65 Newborn puppy

66 Has a balance
67 Petri dish medium

DOWN

1 Tamandua's diet
2 Kind of pepper
3 TV trophy
4 Golf expendable
5 Make certain
6 Martin's screen partner
7 "Serves you right!"
8 Meshed locale
9 Map abbreviation, perhaps
10 Certain cotton-eater
11 Clever thought
12 Supply for play pistols
13 Alternatively
18 Sikorsky or Stravinsky
19 Import duty, e.g.
23 It may be dished
25 Belly laugh
26 Bestow an honor upon
27 New ___, India
28 Director Forman
29 Script direction
30 Guided excursion
31 Others in Mexico
32 Barnyard honker
33 Red Sea country
35 Norse capital
38 Chivalrous Robin
39 Actress Brennan
40 Drifting ice sheet
45 Make someone do something

46 Footballer's footwear
47 Feel pain
49 Concluding dance movement
50 Expression of relief
51 Poison ivy symptom
52 End of many sanctuaries
54 Flintstone's pet

55 Chew on, as a bone
56 Hosiery problem
57 Where Bill Walton played college ball
58 Kind of belly
60 Prognosticator's forte, maybe
61 Eggs, scientifically

EAT FOR INDEPENDENCE

By Arthur Groom

ACROSS
1 Obeys the green light
5 Dummkopfs
10 Charitable offerings
14 First name in a Tolstoy novel
15 Unwelcome kitchen visitor
16 Partiality
17 July 4th entree, perhaps
19 Farm insects
20 Prayer
21 Front-runner
23 Copy machine need
24 Expression of displeasure
26 Hunky-dory
28 Tots give them to get attention
29 Just one of those things?
30 Cum laude modifier
32 Road shape
33 Medium pace
34 Timberland
35 July 4th beverage, perhaps
37 More than whimper
40 Wilderness rarity
41 Snowball of literature
44 Variety of salts
45 Saucy
46 Train-sound syllable
47 Flow stopper
48 Chipmunk snack
50 Wonder Woman alias
51 Trade diplomat
53 Sight in the west
54 Be revolting?
55 July 4th dressing, perhaps

58 Singer Redding
59 Central artery
60 Pointing devices
61 Revolutionary computer game
62 San Francisco player, briefly
63 Years in Madrid

DOWN
1 Inquisition collar
2 Burdensome
3 Many have twists
4 Disrespects verbally
5 Like some cereal
6 Alley-___
7 Atomize
8 Yellow and black cat
9 Shakespearean title character
10 In ___ way (suffering)
11 Family tree
12 Dowagers
13 Bacon sound
18 Neither companion
22 California nut
24 Liquor serving, perhaps
25 One at a wedding reception
27 Krazy of the comics
29 Cream was one
31 Common verb
33 Wendy's pitchman, once
34 Royal decree
35 Reporter's question, often
36 Threadbare
37 You may make it in the morning

38 Lack of transparency
39 Effortless learning procedure
41 Introduce gradually
42 "Rhinoceros" playwright Eugene
43 Chin beards trimmed into a point
45 Hoi follower
46 Movie house

49 Castro, for one
50 "Well, that's completely obvious!"
52 Where worms may be served
53 An unwanted lasting impression
54 CD-___
56 Keats subject
57 Summer, to a Frenchman

THE KETTLES

By Ginger Davis

ACROSS

1 Plows into
5 Like some bank accounts
10 Small apartments, in ads
14 "___ Good Men" (1992)
15 Turkish title of old
16 Fortune 500 abbr.
17 Telepathic, e.g.
19 Type of thermometer
20 Earthquake
21 Parents in this puzzle
23 Barrel part
26 Grier in "The Thing With Two Heads"
27 To ___ (precisely)
31 Lowest male voices
33 Famous London street
36 Bottom lines
41 Assumption, in an argument
42 "The Satanic Verses" author
43 Relishes
44 Continuous scene
45 Disguised, for short
47 World Series sextet
48 Nasal partitions, e.g.
52 Relinquish, as control
55 California observatory site
57 Turkish capital
62 Neighbor of Iran
63 Manuel Noriega, for one
66 Ides words
67 Related to mom
68 Ricelike pasta
69 It has a sole

70 Simpletons
71 Garden crasher

DOWN

1 Spellbound
2 A long way off
3 Word with pittance
4 Started a triathlon
5 Wear proudly
6 Kind of chest or paint
7 Belief system
8 Forms
9 Room in a casa
10 Inexpensive, in product names
11 Henry and Gerald
12 Part of a filmstrip
13 Spread apart, as fingers
18 Anti votes
22 Short vocal solo
24 Not impotent
25 Actor Kilmer
27 Computer programs, briefly
28 "GWTW" domicile
29 Abbr. on a mountain sign
30 "Sesame Street" Muppet
32 Benumb
34 Sister of Moses
35 Org.
37 Traffic sign word
38 First of all?
39 Favor one side?
40 Famous septet
42 More than fume
44 Luau offering

46 First name among those with famous noses
48 Seekers of intelligence?
49 Third rock from the sun
50 Aristotle's teacher
51 Close-fitting woman's hat
53 Shoots in the foot, e.g.
54 Type of testing

56 Followed suit precisely
58 Have memorized
59 Million add-on
60 Level with a bulldozer
61 "___ is as good as a wink"
64 Grab a few winks
65 Lunched or munched

BODY COUNT
By Major Davison

ACROSS

1 Sounds from a milk container?
5 Wraps up
9 Mislead
14 "Robinson Crusoe" locale
15 Tract of wet ground
16 Mirrors companion
17 Dart about
18 Realtor's map
19 Copycats
20 Treat
23 Tit for __
24 Balloon variety
25 V-shaped cut
27 Used extreme subtlety
31 Grief-stricken
34 Half brother of William I
35 Fax forerunner
37 Straightedge
38 Get to one's feet
40 Collar stiffeners
42 Pasta variety
43 "__ is human ..."
45 Sky-bearer of myth
47 Genealogy word
48 Put on
50 Beyond repair
52 Stereotypical dog name
54 Request for help
55 Virgo's predecessor
57 Examine the situation
62 Caribbean vacation destination
64 Animated actor

65 Disappeared
66 Record material
67 Word with onion or friendship
68 Polish prose
69 South American range
70 Bullfight bravos
71 Specified day

DOWN

1 Petulant displeasure
2 Artist Edvard Munch's home
3 Vaudeville shtick
4 Resolve, as a dispute
5 Accentuations
6 Alexandria's location
7 Lacking in liveliness
8 ___ stone (unalterable)
9 Book of hymns
10 Authority at home
11 Behave
12 Beaked pods
13 Egg depository
21 Sound engineer's word
22 Defensive tennis shot
26 Santa ___, Calif.
27 Little kids build them
28 Einstein opposite
29 Snoop
30 "___ of a Salesman"
32 Lavish parties
33 Samples
36 Percussion instrument
39 Therefore
41 Young trees

44 Exposes
46 Caught in the act
49 Algerian title, pre-1830
51 Fell behind
53 Fashionably old-fashioned
55 Molten spew

56 The Emerald Isle
58 Plug away
59 Scotch partner
60 Collegian's credit
61 Banished Rose
63 Toodle-oo

WHOOSH!

By Fran & Lou Sabin

ACROSS

1 Hidey-hole
6 TV morning man
11 Type of tank
14 Has a crick, e.g.
15 Make applicable, as a law
16 Carriage track
17 He'd rather not serve
19 It may be puffed up
20 Parlor piece
21 Hitchcock thriller, 1942
23 Ole's kin
25 Master of irony
26 Items in a smokehouse
30 Milky liquids in some plants
33 Quaker State port
34 Words with the doctor
35 Words with deal or date
38 Flutes, fifes and piccolos
42 One who may make an admission?
43 Nail anagram
44 Pop singer Coolidge
45 Actor Stamp
47 Private vegetable?
48 Withdraw from an organization
51 Stable staple
53 Iranians of yore
56 Airfield builders of WWII
61 Umbrage
62 Proceed effortlessly
64 Brooks Brothers item
65 Time off

66 Make new holes
67 Cry of fright
68 Made a boo-boo
69 Like skid row

DOWN

1 Thersitical fellows
2 Part of the back 40
3 Type of room
4 Weight
5 Acid and alcohol yield
6 Classic roadster
7 They're offensive and chase bombs
8 Smitten
9 Subject of a night raid
10 "Greed" director Erich von
11 New at the game
12 Foreshadow
13 Building part
18 Give a hand
22 Some of the Consumer Reports staff
24 Give a hard time
26 Do an axe job
27 Like the Kara Kum
28 Greedy response
29 Calms down, in a way
31 American missile
32 Add vitamins to, e.g.
36 Editing room sound
37 Aleutian island
39 Unfit for consumption
40 Discomfort

41 In a blue funk, e.g.
46 Mom or dad, traditionally
48 Cause of some grudges
49 Like poltergeists
50 Water source
52 Sentence units
54 A stone's throw away

55 Golfer Ballesteros
57 Craft's position, sometimes
58 Be an omen of
59 ''National Velvet'' author
   Bagnold
60 Like hollandaise sauce
63 London Zoo feature?

HIGH SIGNS

By Joy M. Andrews

ACROSS

1 Noted Washington
6 Kim Jong-il's place
10 Trident-shaped letters
14 It may be present in undercooked meat
15 Like some memories
16 "Alas!"
17 Burton who played Kunta Kinte
18 It may have fallen on a foot
19 Matter to go to court over
20 Idiom for a multitude of ongoing projects
23 Type of part
24 Flat payment?
25 Idiom for the noblest members of society
31 It has its own Web site
32 Indicator of age
33 Were in the present
34 Bar Mitzvah dance
35 Fix
36 1957 Nabokov title
37 Tolkien flesh-eater
38 Fizzles out
40 Forms metal, in a way
42 Idiom for no longer able to function
45 Prexy's associate
46 Publisher who transformed Vogue
47 Idiom for an impracticable dream

53 A famous Fitzgerald
54 Problem of pubescence
55 Pontificate
56 One of 10 leapers in a song
57 Mrs. Dithers
58 Remove the groceries, e.g.
59 Eyelid flare-up
60 Blyton the writer
61 Former Russian sovereigns

DOWN

1 Where cuts might be treated with salt
2 One finishing off the cake
3 De ___ (from the beginning)
4 Five-time Emmy award-winning actor
5 Shaggy like the stereotypical caveman
6 Avidly supporting
7 Start doing laundry
8 Part of a foot
9 Sticks (to)
10 Green stuff on copper
11 Type of missile
12 Hungarian political figure Nagy
13 "Game, ___, match"
21 "Take ___ leave it!"
22 Features of some fancy bathtubs
25 Fern's beginning
26 U.S. Army's helicopter assault division

27 Tear down verbally
28 Participate without the lyrics
29 Judge, e.g.
30 Their teeth are rare
31 Sporting footwear
35 Whirlpool feature
36 Seamstresses' guides
38 Intentionally lay off the fats and sweets
39 Ensconced
40 Flatten a fly

41 Road erosion after a rain, e.g.
43 Infamous marquis
44 Three trios
47 Coagulate
48 Supply-and-demand subj.
49 Cross inscription
50 Rhyme scheme
51 ___-TASS
52 Size category for shirts, briefly
53 Overhead trains

JUST PLAIN FOLKS
By Fran & Lou Sabin

ACROSS
1 Famous brother
5 Woodsy sites, often
10 Nosebag filler
14 "Mon ___!"
15 Papal garb
16 Black fly, e.g.
17 Feathered projectile
18 Squash squasher
19 Having the jitters, perhaps
20 Hit tune by 58-Across
23 Lobster trap
24 Something fishy?
25 Fall back
28 Drags one's feet
31 Liqueur glass
33 ___ War, 1899-1902
35 Raison d'___
36 Hit tune by 58-Across
43 All-conquering thing
44 Rump
45 Helped someone cover up?
49 One beyond belief?
54 Yon maiden fair
55 "Ah, me!"
57 Wabbit hunter
58 Yarrow, Stookey, Travers
62 Smile up a storm
64 Rugged rocks
65 Prospectors' prizes
66 Cut the fat
67 ___ verte (gray-green)
68 Lessor's responsibility
69 Luck's title

70 Three-time PGA champ
71 Some St.-Lo seasons

DOWN
1 Detox center candidate
2 Region of Nigeria
3 More hair-raising
4 "Here and Now" singer, Vandross
5 What a mama's boy needs to cut?
6 Elaborate song for solo voice
7 Like Rambo
8 Entreats earnestly
9 It can be delivered on Sunday
10 Curved molding
11 Indy winner, 1969
12 Game of pursuit
13 Chester White's home
21 Cover story?
22 X-ray relative
26 European capital
27 Propagated
29 One billion years, in astronomy
30 Variety of whale
32 Word in a Marines slogan
34 ER staff
36 Expression of general listlessness
37 Solitaire spot, perhaps
38 Making too much
39 Condition of some paint
40 Yunnan or Keemun, e.g.

41 It may be passed
42 Memorable Merman
46 Make lacework, in a way
47 Votes in
48 McGavin of "Kolchak: The Night Stalker"
50 Crime writer Leonard
51 Turkish hostelry

52 Unflustered
53 Secret meetings
56 Alley mark
59 Award for "60 Minutes"
60 Taj Mahal city
61 Betrayed, in a way
62 Liq. container
63 Romantic or Victorian, e.g.

STRIKE A POSE!

By Latisha Howe

ACROSS

1 Anthem beginning
5 Chest muscles, for short
9 It's seen at the Olympics
14 Added up (to)
15 Jack-in-the-pulpit, e.g.
16 A status symbol
17 Poser
19 State one's views
20 Type of wrestler
21 Reeves of "Speed"
23 ___ del Plata (Argentinean resort)
24 Newly hatched hooter
25 Think quietly and inwardly
27 "Well!"
31 Hive members
32 Help wanted advertisement?
33 First name in masterpieces
35 Filly filler
36 Poser
39 Cutting thrust
41 Cooking fat
42 Insecticide banned since 1972
45 Thinly populated
47 Held by a third party, as money
50 Unventilated
52 1836 battle site
53 Retrieve
54 Fancy footwear, once
57 Flaky mineral
58 Like Wingfield's menagerie

60 Poser
63 Ghastly strange
64 Con ___ (with vigor, in music)
65 Elbow-wrist connector
66 Stallone title role
67 Deadly snakes
68 It may be due, get the point?

DOWN

1 Scottish "Oh my!"
2 "According to what authority?"
3 Vials
4 Naval petty officers
5 Golf standard
6 Composer Satie
7 Quaintly attractive
8 Microscope sample
9 Elaborate decoration
10 One way to take a bough
11 Sustenance
12 Threatens
13 Puts forth effort
18 Dove's domicile
22 Homer's neighbor
24 Fourth qtr. followers
26 Rich soil
28 L.B.J.'s successor
29 Part of R.S.V.P.
30 Listlessness
34 Yemeni port
36 "Blue Suede Shoes" writer Perkins
37 Preoccupied with

38 Hwy.
39 Pitchman
40 Served raw
42 Blood count?
43 They may be eminent
44 Tangoing number
45 Drooped
46 Medium's method
48 Kind of old story

49 Coterie
51 Brazilian dance
55 Seafarers
56 Cutting sound
59 A Caesar
61 Calculator figs.
62 First name among legendary crooners

MIRACULOUS CONVERSION
By Arthur Groom

ACROSS

1 Verse with 17 syllables
6 Sentence necessity, often
10 Swedish pop quartet
14 Some woodwinds
15 Biologist's medium
16 Think ahead
17 Miraculous event (Part 1)
20 They may be rolled over
21 Happenings
22 Common possessive
25 "The Republic" author
28 Keats, notably
29 Miraculous event (Part 2)
32 Was genuinely concerned
33 Rousing cheer
34 Ritzy
38 Was acquainted with
39 Decorator's decision
41 Certain Major Leaguer of old
42 Stitched
43 Just fine
44 Mattress innards
45 Miraculous event (Part 3)
48 Malarkey
52 Hardly lenient
53 UFO crew
54 Makes reparation
56 Archaic exclamation
58 Miraculous event (Part 4)
64 Suckling spot
65 29th state
66 Ski lift aids
67 White-tailed eagle
68 Tactic
69 Tree with fluttering leaves

DOWN

1 Today, in Madrid
2 Classification system for blood
3 Debt memo
4 Type of military cap
5 Taken wrong?
6 Medieval menial
7 Often inflated item
8 Country butter?
9 Born and ___
10 Ladybug's lunch
11 Small light pancakes
12 Hunting sounds
13 Brooding worry
18 Powder substance
19 Palindromic sound effect
22 2006 American Idol
23 Illogical
24 Spread by scattering
26 Handyman's gear
27 Middle of Czechoslovakia?
30 Chopped
31 Always, poetically
34 Lowly worker
35 Word with zinc
36 Hightailed it
37 Entertaining folks
39 Raven's response
40 Amazed outcries
44 Card game like rummy
45 Sunday utterance

46 Room to maneuver
47 Thus
48 Waste-maker of adage
49 Significant person?
50 Islamic sacred text (Var.)
51 Tie the knot
55 One way to get to elementary school

57 Kid's claim
59 Fa-la link on a musical scale
60 Number in a Dickens title
61 Laser-gun sound effect
62 Poet's ''before''
63 Nine-digit ID

WHAT'S IN A NAME?

By Fran & Lou Sabin

ACROSS

1 Skewered fare (Var.)
6 Yet again
10 Skelton forte
14 Butler's love
15 Red Cross supplies
16 Fanzine focus
17 "Lover" lyricist
19 Many limo riders
20 Salon application
21 Willie and Joe's carrier
22 Fuel choice
24 Food fishes
25 Carpet-layer's concern
26 Skips the shower?
29 Some may be junior or technical
33 Stage backdrop
34 Monte Carlo action
35 Time co-founder
36 Farsighted one
37 Trattoria sauce
38 Abandon, in a way
39 Substitute for the unnamed
40 James who sings the blues
41 Keyboard key
42 Lessenings of tension between nations
44 Cavern
45 Rank
46 Rue de la ___
47 Vegas employee
50 Wordsmith, of a sort
51 Pre-kiss promise

54 Olympian Korbut
55 Singer of "All I Wanna Do"
58 Cultivated land
59 Sound on a 58-Across, perhaps
60 Chip away at
61 Dieter's problem
62 Clears, on a pay stub
63 Ecclesiastical council

DOWN

1 Far from loving
2 Swabby's salute
3 Unadorned
4 Tram filler
5 Some plunkers' axes
6 Fire proof?
7 Tide type
8 Leave the straight and narrow
9 Decisive defeat
10 "Back to the Future" star
11 Inventor's "light bulb"
12 Night light
13 Where starter
18 Last letters in Lincolnshire
23 ___ Aviv
24 "Essays of Elia" author
25 Arterial trunk
26 Located
27 Glacial ridge
28 Part of a holiday phrase
29 Selects the dramatis personae
30 Jury's determination, perhaps
31 Fancy display

32 Heated conflict
34 Threw a party for
37 Oscar on the 88s
41 Holds back
43 Word on some French gravestones
44 Industrial Indiana city
46 Does a valet's job
47 Tip, as a hat

48 Ben Gurion lander
49 Shah Jahan built here
50 Misshapen
51 Monopoly token
52 Airhead
53 Ran a tab
56 Move apace
57 One way to express joy

FROSTY RECEPTION

By Irma Afram

ACROSS

1 Speakeasy risk
5 Diminish in intensity
10 Strives for victory
14 Christiania today
15 Gale's teammate Piccolo
16 Broadway opening?
17 Sign of fright
19 "All in the Family" producer
20 Aquarium attractions
21 Good to down
23 "Suffice ___ say ..."
24 Become unsteady applying lipstick
25 Kitchen implements
28 Presidential advisory groups
31 Became an issue
32 You might take it lying down
33 Poi base
34 Become cohesive
35 Send in different directions
38 Cassis-flavored aperitif
39 They can be made to meet
41 Blackjack components
42 Showing expertise
44 Took the long way home
46 Stock holders?
47 Big name at Indy
48 Word with stone or storm
49 Noble partner?
51 Train trailers
55 Sommer of "The Prize"
56 Line drive, in baseball lingo
58 Assist in malfeasance

59 Kind of garments
60 Brickell or Falco
61 Basker's beams
62 Baby Moses was hidden among them
63 Plunder

DOWN

1 Enormous fabled birds
2 "A Hard Road to Glory" author
3 Dorsal bones
4 Movers' helpers
5 Brothers' keepers?
6 Shoe designer Magli
7 Draws a bead on, e.g.
8 Percussive dance
9 Touring company
10 Prince of the comics
11 Get-acquainted soiree, e.g.
12 Roster-truncating abbr.
13 Word fit for a king
18 British measures
22 "God" in Latin
24 Bath add-ins, sometimes
25 Flew off the handle
26 "Granny" Ryan
27 One way to quit
28 Quoted as an authority
29 Folderol
30 Particular kinds
32 Certain track auto
36 Likes a lot
37 Give one to a customer, e.g.

40 Shakespearean output
43 Name in the title of a Stephen King best seller
45 Get some good out of
46 They're rattled as a show of force
48 Humiliated on campus, in a way
49 One of a storied threesome
50 Goya's ''The Duchess of ___''
51 Sheep's shelter
52 Word with baking or diet
53 ''The Ten Commandments,'' for one
54 Second part of a kid's game
57 Regret bitterly

1

R	A	M	B	O		A	B	E	T		D	A	R	N
A	H	E	A	D		L	A	N	E		A	L	O	E
N	A	R	R	O	W	I	N	G	C	I	R	C	L	E
		D	R	A	B			H	A	R	O	L	D	
L	E	E		D	I	V	A		N	O	V	E	L	
I	N	D	E	C	I	S	I	V	E		W	E	R	E
D	O	N	N	A		T	E	S	T					
	L	A	D	Y	I	S	A	S	Q	U	A	R	E	
			S	K	I	M			B	L	A	K	E	
S	A	L	E		E	T	I	Q	U	E	T	T	E	S
A	L	A	N	S		S	N	U	G		A	S	S	
N	O	G	G	I	N		A	L	T	O				
T	H	E	I	R	O	N	T	R	I	A	N	G	L	E
E	A	R	N		R	O	A	R		S	T	A	I	R
E	S	S	E		A	R	T	Y		K	O	R	E	A

2

M	A	T	E		S	P	A	S	M		S	I	G	H
A	X	I	S		P	E	K	O	E		K	N	E	E
R	E	S	T	A	U	R	A	N	T	B	I	L	L	S
		A	L	D	O		N	E	O		E	A	T	
E	L	A	T	E		R	A	E		C	U	T	T	O
D	I	R	E	C	T	A	T	T	A	C	K	S	O	N
G	E	M		S	A	T	E		G	E	E			
E	N	Y	A		B	E	L	L	E		S	O	R	E
	L	A	O		I	O	N	A		T	A	G		
A	N	O	P	P	O	N	E	N	T	S	K	I	N	G
D	E	C	O	R		O	R	G		P	E	S	T	S
O	W	E		O	A	R		S	T	E	T			
B	A	L	A	N	C	E	S	P	A	R	T	N	E	R
E	G	O	S		T	E	E	U	P		L	A	K	E
S	E	T	H		S	N	A	R	E		E	Y	E	D

3

A	R	A	R	A	T		L	I	E		S	T	Y	E
R	E	N	E	G	E		L	I	N	O	L	E	U	M
M	A	N	D	A	N		D	I	S	R	A	E	L	I
S	P	E	C	I	E	S		C	I	D	E	R		
		A	N	T	I	C		B	A	N				
S	C	A	R	S		C	O	M	A	S		H	I	P
T	E	M	P	T	S		V	A	N		F	A	R	E
I	D	E	E		A	R	E	N	A		L	I	K	E
L	E	N	T		V	A	T		L	O	O	T	E	R
E	S	S		N	E	W	E	R		V	O	I	D	S
			E	O	S		D	O	T	T	E	R		
H	E	A	T	H		T	A	R	T	E	S	T		
I	C	E	H	O	U	S	E		R	A	I	D	E	R
T	H	R	O	W	R	U	G		O	G	L	A	L	A
S	O	Y	S		N	E	O		S	E	E	M	L	Y

4

A	R	C	S		T	A	R	P		L	A	Z	E	S
S	O	U	L		O	L	I	O		O	N	E	A	L
A	B	B	E		B	L	O	C	K	P	A	R	T	Y
P	S	E	U	D	O		J	O	E	S		O	I	L
		S	T	I	G	M	A		P	I	G	S	T	Y
O	N	T	H	E	G	O		V	I	D	A			
B	E	E	S		A	U	T	O		E	L	B	O	W
E	R	A		A	N	N	O	Y	E	D		O	D	E
Y	O	K	E	L		D	E	A	N		E	X	I	T
			O	L	E	S		G	L	A	N	C	E	S
O	P	E	N	E	R		G	E	I	S	H	A		
L	I	L		G	L	E	E		S	H	A	M	E	S
S	Q	U	A	R	E	K	N	O	T		N	E	M	O
O	U	T	D	O		E	I	R	E		C	R	I	B
N	E	E	D	S		D	E	E	D		E	A	R	S

152

Puzzle 5

F	D	R	■	M	O	S	S	Y	■	L	U	F	F	S
O	R	A	■	G	R	O	P	E	■	A	N	I	L	E
C	A	T	A	M	A	R	A	N	■	S	I	S	A	L
A	M	E	N	■	■	N	E	T	S	■	E	T	H	Y	L
L	A	D	I	N	G	■	■	■	T	R	E	E	■	
■	■	M	A	E	S	T	R	O	S	■	R	A	P	
R	A	B	A	T	■	L	O	A	M	■	A	M	O	R
E	M	I	T	■	F	A	R	C	E	■	B	A	N	E
D	I	R	E	■	O	M	S	K	■	C	O	N	E	Y
O	D	D	■	R	E	S	I	S	T	O	R	■		
■	B	A	A	S	■	■	A	T	T	A	I	N		
D	O	R	M	S	■	A	T	O	P	■	E	R	G	O
U	N	A	P	T	■	D	O	G	P	A	D	D	L	E
S	T	I	L	E	■	E	R	R	E	D	■	E	O	N
T	O	N	E	R	■	S	E	E	D	S	■	N	O	D

5

Puzzle 6

O	A	F	S	■	M	A	C	O	N	■	S	T	A	G
C	R	E	E	■	A	L	A	N	A	■	T	A	R	O
C	I	T	R	I	C	A	C	I	D	■	O	B	I	E
U	S	E	R	S	■	S	H	O	E	■	O	L	D	S
R	E	S	A	L	E	■	E	N	R	A	G	E	■	
■	T	E	L	L	■	■	■	■	C	E	S	A	R	
L	I	C	E	■	L	A	T	H	E	R	■	A	L	E
I	D	A	■	M	E	T	H	A	N	E	■	L	E	A
E	O	N	■	U	N	S	E	L	D	■	S	T	E	P
F	L	E	E	T	■	■	L	E	F	T	■			
■	S	A	T	U	R	N	■	D	R	E	A	M	S	
T	A	U	T	■	P	E	A	T	■	O	P	R	A	H
U	R	G	E	■	B	A	K	I	N	G	S	O	D	A
R	E	A	R	■	O	T	E	R	O	■	O	M	A	N
N	A	R	Y	■	W	A	D	E	R	■	N	A	M	E

6

Puzzle 7

B	U	S	T	S	■	E	L	F	■	W	E	A	R	E
I	N	T	R	A	■	M	E	R	■	I	R	V	I	N
G	L	E	A	M	■	M	A	A	■	N	E	O	N	S
T	A	P	I	O	C	A	P	U	D	D	I	N	G	
O	C	U	L	A	R	■	D	U	G	■				
P	E	P	■	A	O	L	■	M	A	T	Z	O	S	
■	J	I	G	S	A	W	P	U	Z	Z	L	E		
O	N	I	O	N	■	S	R	I	■	G	A	Z	E	R
H	O	R	A	T	I	O	A	L	G	E	R			
S	W	E	D	E	N	■	S	E	A	■	M	S	G	
■	R	N	S	■	R	A	P	I	E	R				
D	I	S	C	O	M	B	O	B	U	L	A	T	E	
R	U	P	E	E	■	A	I	M	■	R	A	S	T	A
E	A	S	E	D	■	S	K	A	■	A	C	M	E	S
B	L	O	K	E	■	H	E	N	■	L	E	A	R	Y

7

Puzzle 8

R	A	G	E	■	S	C	A	B	S	■	C	L	A	N
A	B	E	L	■	M	O	D	E	M	■	H	O	L	T
F	R	O	M	H	A	N	D	T	O	M	O	U	T	H
F	O	R	S	A	L	E	■	A	T	O	P	■		
L	A	G	■	P	L	Y	■	T	E	N	■	C	A	D
E	D	E	N	■	S	H	E	■	S	C	A	P	E	
■	E	S	P	■	I	S	O	T	O	P	E	S		
H	I	G	H	O	F	F	T	H	E	H	O	G		
D	I	S	R	A	E	L	I	■	O	R	E			
O	D	E	O	N	■	U	S	E	■	N	E	L	L	
N	E	E	■	N	I	X	■	O	P	T	■	N	E	O
■	T	O	N	I	■	C	O	A	L	G	A	S		
B	E	Y	O	N	D	O	N	E	S	M	E	A	N	S
A	R	E	A	■	I	N	A	N	E	■	A	G	E	E
S	A	N	D	■	A	S	T	E	R	■	F	E	D	S

8

SOLUTION KEY

Puzzle 9

S	L	A	N	G		L	I	R	A		I	B	A	R
O	U	S	E	L		A	D	O	S		M	U	S	E
O	S	S	I	A		B	O	O	T	C	A	M	P	S
T	H	U	N	D	E	R	S	T	R	U	C	K		
H	E	M		I	L	E		B	O	B		N	U	T
E	R	E		O	R	A	T	E		S	E	E	P	S
		A	L	E		H	E	H		T	E	A	K	
	R	A	I	N	F	O	R	E	S	T	S			
U	T	A	H		O	R	R		B	T	U			
N	O	M	S	G		I	N	T	R	A		G	I	T
D	E	B		A	C	T		R	O	N		R	N	A
	L	I	G	H	T	N	I	N	G	F	A	S	T	
O	V	E	R	S	L	E	E	P		E	A	T	A	T
N	O	O	K		O	R	A	L		T	R	I	N	E
O	W	N	S		E	S	T	E		Z	O	N	E	D

9

Puzzle 10

B	A	C	H		A	P	E	S		S	P	R	E	E
R	I	L	E		R	U	T	H		P	E	E	V	E
O	L	O	F		E	R	A	T		A	R	D	E	N
W	E	N	T	B	A	L	L	I	S	T	I	C		
S	E	E	Y	A			C	H	E		L	B	S	
E	N	D		S	L	I	N	K	Y		F	O	A	L
			M	A	O	R	I		A	R	U	B	A	
G	O	T	A	L	L	S	T	E	A	M	E	D	U	P
A	D	U	L	T			T	E	N	E	T			
L	O	G	E		S	P	I	R	A	L		Y	E	A
S	R	O		D	E	L					I	C	I	N	G
			F	L	E	W	I	N	T	O	A	R	A	G	E
N	O	W	I	N		G	O	O	P		A	S	I	N
O	R	A	L	S		H	A	F	T		W	O	N	T
T	O	R	T	E		T	H	U	S		S	U	E	S

10

Puzzle 11

H	I	R	E	S		A	C	H	E		G	O	B	I
E	N	O	C	H		G	O	O	D		A	R	I	D
A	S	T	H	E	W	O	R	L	D	T	U	R	N	S
V	E	T	O		A	R	A	M	A	I	C			
E	R	E		O	R	A	L		L	H	A	S	A	
S	T	R	A	P	S		A	L	L	O	V	E	R	
		L	E	H	A	V	R	E			I	V	E	
	O	N	E	L	I	F	E	T	O	L	I	V	E	
S	D	I		P	R	E	S	T	O	N				
P	I	C	A	S	S	O		A	N	N	A	L	S	
A	N	K	L	E		C	A	R	E		B	E	T	
		T	E	N	F	O	L	D		W	A	V	Y	
G	E	N	E	R	A	L	H	O	S	P	I	T	A	L
E	V	E	R		B	E	E	N		I	R	E	N	E
T	E	E	S		S	A	N	G		T	E	S	T	S

11

Puzzle 12

S	A	V	A	G	E		N	A	M		F	A	D	S
I	N	A	W	A	Y		A	C	E		O	N	E	O
L	O	C	A	L	E		N	A	T	I	O	N	A	L
O	N	U	S		W	A	S	H	S	T	A	N	D	
			U	H	H	U	H		T	O	N	S		
D	O	M		E	P	I	C		D	O	O	D	L	E
A	C	T		S	O	N	I	A		T	R	U	E	R
T	O	U	R		N	E	A	T	O		E	S	A	U
E	M	B	E	R		D	O	L	L	Y		T	S	P
S	E	E	S	A	W		S	A	G	E		J	E	T
			O	B	I	E		S	A	N	T	A		
S	C	R	U	B	S	U	I	T		E	C	H	O	
C	O	U	R	I	E	R	S		W	A	L	K	U	P
O	P	E	C		T	O	M		A	L	L	E	G	E
W	A	D	E		O	S	S		R	E	S	T	E	D

12

154

13

```
P S S T   W O R K   C A N E S
A M A H   I V A N   O D E L L
W E R E   R E N O   N O R M A
  W A S H I N G T O N P O S T
      P A N S Y   N E T
C A R I N G   S E C   D E L
A R E A   K A P U T   R A E
J O H N P H I L I P S O U S A
U M A   L O D E N   L I E S
N A B   A N D   P A D D L E
    E N D   C R U S T
H A I L T O T H E C H I E F
A B O V E   H O N K   M U L L
N E W E R   A R T E   E R I E
G L A S S   W E A R   R O P E
```

14

```
A R G O   B L O A T   J A R S
D E R M   L I N G O   U H O H
A S A P   U N C A P   D A M E
M O T H E R T E R E S A
S W E A R B Y   L I T U P
    L O S   M A M A C A S S
I M T O O   M A L A Y   L A H
A A H S   M A M M Y   T O G A
M R I   L O A M S   R E N E W
B I G M O M M A   D I M
S A H I B   A R T E M I S
  M O M M Y D E A R E S T
A S T O   G O U D A   I D L E
M A R S   R U L E R   T E A M
A P I A   S E E D Y   Y A M S
```

15

```
H A F T   A C R E   C S P A N
O R E O   P O O L   O C H R E
H O T E L R O O M   D O O N E
U M A   A O L   F I T T E D
M A L I G N   P R O N T O
    N O S E R I N G   C O M
P E S T O   T O O T   B O L E
E L L E N   H O T   P O P I N
N E I L   S A F E   A S Y O U
D E N   G E N E R O U S
    G R A T E D   I N A R U T
R I S E R S   T L C   A N A
O O H E D   P S Y C H O T I C
S T O V E   C O P A   B O O K
E A T E N   S T E N   I N N S
```

16

```
B A A S   I N R E   D I S C O
A L M A   D O I N   E L C I D
S T I L L L I F E   B L O N D
T O R T O I S E   B A S T E S
    L O N E   C R U E T
E D G I N G   P R I C E T A G
M E R C Y   D O U G H   U M A
B E A K   C U R D S   C R A M
E R S   D A N C E   S H O N E
R E S E A R C H   L E E W A Y
    S L I D E   C O R E
T O T A L S   C H A I R M A N
O K A P I   C L I F F F A C E
A R I S E   D O L E   U N I T
D A N E S   S T I R   L E D S
```

17

```
R A N K   N A R C S   R O M E
O M E N   A P A R T   A L I A
T A R E   M E T O O   K A N T
C H I E F E X E C U T I V E S
      L I D     T E N
P O S S E   S D S   A G L O W
A M A   R E T A K E   I O L E
P E T T Y G R I E V A N C E S
A G U E   O I L I E R   K I T
L A P E L   A Y N   E V E N S
      N A T     S T E
O F F I C E R M A T E R I A L
M I R E   M E A R A   N O V A
A L A S   P A G E I   O T I C
R E N T   T R I A D   N A V Y
```

18

```
M A L A   S E I S M   A N O N
A S A S   T O N K A   R O M A
C H I C K E N R U N   B R I M
H E R O N   I N I T I A T E
U N S T O P S   K A R T
      T I E S   C A R A F E
A M I S   T R E K   C A R E T
D U C K T A I L H A I R C U T
A N E Y E   F L A X   Y O D A
M I D W A Y   S K I N
      A S E A   I S O L A T E
V I O L E N C E   S A C H S
A M O K   T U R K E Y T R O T
N E N E   A T I L T   T I N E
S T A R   S E E M S   E D G E
```

19

```
L E E R   S C R A M   A L A S
U R G E   T H U L E   R I C E
C O R P O R A T E L A D D E R
A D E   P E T S   J E S S E
S E T T E E S   A L A N
      A N T   F L I R T I N G
S H E L L   G A L A   D O E
E A R L Y R E T I R E M E N T
A L I   A N T E   R I S E S
T E N A C I T Y   T O N
      N O D S   M I T T E N S
A R B O R   S A R I   L O P
G O L D E N P A R A C H U T E
E P E E   O I L E D   E D E N
S E W S   G E E S E   N E S T
```

20

```
S E T H   D A S H   F L O G
A C H E   I S L E S   L I S A
W H A L E S H A R K   O L A V
N O R D I C   B O A   T A K E
      U G L I   E T H I C A L
E L E P H A N T S E A L
G O D   T I D E   P L A T E
G O N E   M O R A L   A M I D
S P A N S   S C A N   O L D
      S P I D E R M O N K E Y
M I S N A M E   E A S E
A S I A   O V A   S E A B E D
U S E R   F O X T E R R I E R
L U G E   F I L E R   E L L A
S E E D   D E N Y   R E S T
```

21

| A E S O P | O M O O | A B U T |
| D R I V E | N O U S | S O H O |
| D I V E I N T O T H E P O O L |
S E A R	E A R S	L E T H E
A S A P	I C O N
D E C L A R E I D O	S O A P
A T O L L S	S E T A	C R U
T U L S A	A L S	U T T E R
E D O	S O N E	G R E E C E
S E R T	A T T H E A L T A R
A I R E	A L E E
A L A M O	A C T I	T A T A
G I V E U P T H E D A Y J O B
A M E S	R E A R	S P A R E
R E S T	O R T S	P E R E S

22

E V E S	K E V I N	C R A B
P I T Y	A R E N T	H O B O
I V A N	I R I S H L I N E N
C O L O S S A L	U N I T E
P O E T	A H S O
W E L S H R A B B I T	S R S
H E L I O	A L L S	P I T
E R A S	B E S E T	J I V E
A I M	M A G I	S O R E R
T E A	E N G L I S H H O R N
O D D S	N E O N
E N N U I	B A R E B A C K
S C O T C H T A P E	U R A L
M A U D	M A R I N	L I R E
E R N O	S P R E E	L A T E

23

A P S E	P E R M S	J O A N
B E A T	A D I E U	U N D O
C A P A N D G O W N	D E E S
G O R E	D R E S S Y
S E V E R E	S P R E A D
A L A R M S	Q U I P	I L L
F I L E S	C U R E S	P O E
E X E S	G U A R D	C L O P
S I D	H A R R S	C R O N E
T R I	E S S E	R O O M E R
C E L L E D	E S S A Y S
T A T A M I	A R T S
I G O R	G R A D U A T I O N
C U R L	H U M A N	I N D O
K E Y S	T E A M S	E K E D

24

F R E T S	M A L T	C A S H
E E R I E	E W E R	O N T O
M A N T A	D A V Y J O N E S
M R S O L E A R Y	E L A T E
E S T	A X L E	H A S P
A N T S	T E N	O F F
L A R G E R	W H I S T L E R
O L I O	U S H E R	R I T E
A V O G A D R O	L E A S E D
N A G	L E I	P O N Y
R U B S	M O O G	S U M
A G A T E	H A M M U R A B I
M O N T E Z U M A	L I M O S
M A D E	A R I D	F L O A T
O D E R	G L E E	S L A T S

25

```
D I R T . I N N S . Q U O T A
I D E A . N O O K . U N T I L
T A L L . T O R I . A T I L T
C H I C K E N A N D R I C E .
H O C . O N E . C I T E . . .
. . A R T . R O D S . F U N .
I R E N E . A I L S . S O S O
M E A T A N D P O T A T O E S
P A S S . A V E R . D A D D Y
S P Y . A M I N . A I R . . .
. . E W E S . I T E . S P A .
. B R E A D A N D B U T T E R
H O U R I . B A L E . H A R E
A D M I T . L I E S . A L M A
T Y P E S . E R S T . N E S S
```

26

```
F E R R I S . T A M P . D N A
A R O U S E . A F R O . R O W
W E A T H E R C A S T . I L L
N I N A . K E I R . H A L L S
. . . B R E S T . D E L L . .
A F F A I R E . M I R A C L E
G R E G G . A C E R B . H I S
N E V A . C R E A K . B U T S
E Y E . B A C O N . S U C R E
W A R P A T H . T H I C K E N
. . P U B S . K I O S K . . .
R A I N Y . D E M I . S I L K
A R T . S T O N E S T H R O W
S I C . A W E D . T R O I K A
H A H . T A R O . S I T S I N
```

27

```
M E S A . A B A S H . E C H O
E R O S . S E R U M . L O A F
M I L K S H A K E S . N E R F
O C A . A R T . R I N K S . .
. A R E N A . C S P A N . . .
P L Y M O U T H R O C K S . .
S L O M O . P R U D E . O N E
H O W S . R E A P S . G R E W
I C E . B U N C O . L I N E N
V I R G I N I A R E E L S . .
. L O T T O . T H A T S . . .
E L V I S . C H A . A A A . .
B E E T . J E L L Y R O L L S
A N T Z . O N E A L . S K E W
N O S Y . B E E P S . E S M E
```

28

```
P R O D S . W R A P . A P S E
R E P A Y . H A R E . L A U D
I C E B R E A K E R . T S P S
S E N S I B L E . M O T E . .
O D E . A B E . T A U . R R S
N E R O . R E A P S . A M I .
. . A L A . P L A C E M A T .
. W A T E R M O C C A S I N .
B A L S A M I C . E T A . . .
E X T . D E L H I . U R G E .
G P A . E D O . G O B . A O L
A M E R . M U H A M M A D . .
U P O N . S T E A M T A B L E
M E N D . S E A N . E L L I S
A R T S . N A D A . S L E E T
```

29

P	E	G	S		M	A	M	A		T	W	A	I	N
O	R	A	N		T	H	O	U		H	E	N	N	A
M	O	V	E	O	V	E	R	D	A	R	L	I	N	G
A	D	I	E	U		M	A	I	L	E	D			
D	E	A	R	T	H		Y	O	D	A		H	O	P
E	S	L		D	A	B		O	T	T	A	W	A	
		S	I	L	E	N	T		H	U	L	L		
	H	E	A	D	O	V	E	R	H	E	E	L	S	
K	I	E	V		Y	E	O	M	A	N				
A	L	L	E	G	E		D	O	S		F	I	G	
Y	O	S		A	L	O	E		S	T	E	R	N	E
	S	L	E	D	G	E		E	V	I	T	A		
M	O	O	N	O	V	E	R	P	A	R	A	D	O	R
O	N	A	I	R		T	E	E	M		D	A	N	E
B	E	T	T	E		S	T	E	P		E	Y	E	D

30

I	G	O	R		T	A	B	L	E		A	G	H	A
M	U	S	T		U	B	O	A	T		P	L	A	Y
P	E	T	E	R	L	O	R	R	E		R	A	Z	E
A	R	E		A	L	A	N	S		H	I	D	E	S
C	R	A	S	H	E	R		B	A	L	I			
T	E	L	L		D	E	B	A	R		O	R	C	
		S	M		V	A	N	D	A	L	I	C		
L	O	N	C	H	A	N	E	Y	J	U	N	I	O	R
A	W	A	K	E	N	E	R		O	P	S			
B	E	T		R	O	O	T	S		O	S	L	O	
	U	S	P	S		P	O	I	N	T	E	R		
M	A	R	I	A		C	A	R	G	O		R	A	G
I	R	A	N		B	E	L	A	L	U	G	O	S	I
T	A	L	C		A	R	E	T	E		I	D	E	E
E	L	S	E		S	T	E	T	S		N	E	S	S

31

Z	E	T	A		R	A	G	S		E	L	D	S	
E	T	A	L		O	V	U	M		D	I	A	N	A
A	U	R	A		T	I	M	E	P	I	E	C	E	S
L	I	P	R	E	A	D		L	L	C		H	E	P
		M	E	T		F	L	A	T	C	A	R	S	
A	L	L	C	L	E	A	R		I	S	H			
B	O	I	L	S		H	O	R	N		R	A	T	S
C	O	C	O		M	A	L	E	S		O	B	O	E
S	P	E	C		I	B	I	D		I	N	E	R	T
		K	E	N		C	O	R	R	O	D	E	S	
P	E	A	S	A	N	T	S		A	I	M			
A	R	M		S	O	O		A	S	S	E	R	T	S
W	R	I	S	T	W	A	T	C	H		T	A	R	A
L	E	T	H	E		D	A	R	E		E	N	O	S
D	Y	E	R		S	U	E	S		R	I	D	S	

32

R	O	G	E	T		S	T	E	T		S	C	A	N
A	P	N	E	A		C	A	V	E		P	A	R	E
T	E	A	R	J	E	R	K	E	R		A	S	I	A
A	N	T	I		S	E	I	N	E		W	H	A	T
		E	A	T	E	N		S	A	N	D			
A	D	O		B	E	N		D	A	D		R	A	P
L	A	V	O	I	S	I	E	R		D	H	A	B	I
O	D	E	L	L		N	E	E		I	O	W	A	N
H	O	R	D	E		G	L	A	S	S	I	E	S	T
A	S	H		N	Y	S		R	H	O		R	E	S
		A	R	E	A		L	I	E	N	S			
S	L	U	E		H	E	I	N	E		O	U	S	T
C	O	L	A		W	I	R	E	P	U	L	L	E	R
A	B	E	D		E	R	A	S		L	A	N	A	I
B	O	D	E		H	E	S	S		T	R	A	M	S

33

| D Y E S | | P U P A L | | M O R T |
| E A R N | | A G I L E | | A L A R |
| C L E A N T H E L A T R I N E |
A L I F E		D O V E C O T E
	U S M C		Y E N	
C A P		S E A L		S E N S E S
U S E D		A C E S		T E T R A
S C R U B T H E M I S S I O N
P O K E R		E K E D		T E S T
S T Y L A R		S A L E		S E A
	Y E S		R E D D	
A C H I E V E S		A R U B A
L A U N D E R T H E M O N E Y
D I R K		A V A I L		N I N E
O N L Y		L E N D S		E X E S

34

B E G S		R A Z E S		J A D E
L U R E		E D E M A		A V O W
O R A L		L O R I S		V I S E
C O F F E E P O T S		A D E S
	V A T		E M S	
A L I C E S		F O R E C A S T
T Y R A		E N I D		T R U L Y
R O O F		S E L I G		I D O L
I N N E R		A L E E		P I P E
A S S A U L T S		N A T T E R
	U N I		S I R	
C A L L		C A P P U C C I N O
A R I A		K I L O S		O D O R
S A K I		E D U C E		A L O E
A B E T		D E S K S		L E N S

35

A S S N		A T L A S		O D O R
I T O O		B O O T H		M E M O
D Y A N		J U R O R		A L A S
E X P O S U R E M A C H I N E
	M R S		P E A	
C O L L I E		J U N O		I C E
A X I A L		C U T E		D R U M
P I E C E T R I A L F R A M E
E D G E		R I C H		L A T I N
S E E		M O B Y		L E G E N D
	P E P		T O E	
Z O N E L I N E W A R P O U T
E V I L		C A B I N		E A S E
R E N T		A T O N E		S H E A
O R E S		L O N E R		T U R K

36

| A S H Y | | B E G A T | | C O P S |
| L E O I | | R E E S E | | A R E A |
| G E N E R A L A S S E M B L Y |
A N K L E		R E L A P S E S
	D U N S		T A R	
R C A		P E T S		S L O W U P
A R M S		M A T E		O V A L S
B E E T H O V E N S F I F T H
I M B U E		E A V E		S E R A
D E A D L Y		D O E R		R A W
	L A P		I D E A	
A C A D E M E S		A R G O T
C O L O R A D O S P R I N G S
H A M S		H A I T I		S A R A
E L S E		A L L A N		E W E R

37

```
L E A C H . A C T O R . R O W
E A G L E . S H A R E . E R R
G R E E N T H U M B S . A D E
O S S A . A C R E . E L L E N
. . N O L A N . S A Y E R S .
B R A S S K N U C K L E S . .
L I B E L . P O I . S T E P
I L L . O A F . O D D . A V A
P L E A . S E A . O A T E S .
. . B U T T E R F I N G E R S
V O O D O O . R O S S I . . .
I N D I A . P E R P . T A X I
T R I . S W E A T Y P A L M S
A Y E . T O R R E . A T S E A
L E D . S E U S S . L O O N Y
```

38

```
A N G U S . D R U B . B A Y S
L E A P T . R E N O . A L O E
S A M O A . A D E N . N O U N
O P E N I N G D A Y . N U N S
. . . R U N E S . H E D G E .
G O E S . R E N E G E R . . .
U N T W I S T S . R I Y A D H
A C C E D E S . L O R E L E I
R E H E A R . P A S S A B L E
. . . P H Y S I C S . R A I D
S A Y S O . H E E L S . . . .
C R O W . M E R R Y M O N T H
O G L E . U R S A . A D O B E
L U K E . S P O T . R E R A N
D E S K . S A N E . T S A R S
```

39

```
A S S E S . T O F U . U S D A
C O U R T . U N I T . P L U S
M O V I E . E X T R A . R A N T
E N S N A R E . S H O O T E R
. . M A D E . L A S S O . . .
A N N A . S O L D I E R . . .
L E A S E . D A T A . L E I
M A R I N E R E S E R V I S T
S T Y . D O E R . Y E A T S
. . B U N D L E S . T R A Y
C H A I R . Y A K S . . . .
R E G R E T S . S I T U A T E
E N I D . B A B Y S I T T E R
E R L E . A G O G . R E R A N
D Y E R . R E P O . S P A R E
```

40

```
C A R T E . S T O M P . T W O
O R I E L . C I L I A . R I D
P E A C E T R E A T Y . A D O
R A N . G E E S . L O N E R
A S T A I R E . D O O R S .
. B E A N I E B A B I E S .
B A L E S . N E E D . E R E
A L O T . C A D D Y . K N I T
R E V . G O B I . D A T E S
B E E T L E B A I L E Y . .
. B E A D Y . D E T O U R S
A L I E N . K L E E . B I T
W A R . C O R N E R S T O N E
A N D . E T H E R . T E A S E
Y E S . S T O W S . S A T E D
```

41

W	A	F	T	S		W	E	A	R		A	B	B	E
H	A	I	R	S		A	R	L	O		R	E	E	L
O	R	L	E	S		D	R	I	L	L	T	E	A	M
S	E	E	P		L	E	A		L	A	I	R	D	S
		F	A	D	E		T	U	S	K	S			
A	N	O	N	Y	M	O	U	S		E	T	H	O	S
S	A	L		N	O	R	M	A			S	A	L	E
S	O	D		E	N	D		B	E	E		M	E	N
A	M	E	S		E	C	L	A	T		M	O	D	
M	I	R	E	S		A	L	E	R	T	N	E	S	S
		A	I	S	L	E		L	E	E	R			
S	P	O	N	G	E		A	N	Y		S	H	A	W
P	U	N	C	H	L	I	N	E		S	T	E	N	O
A	R	T	E		L	O	S	S		E	L	A	T	E
R	E	O	S		S	U	E	S		C	E	D	E	S

42

T	A	P	A	S		S	O	U	P		C	Z	A	R
A	R	I	S	E		A	P	S	O		R	I	C	O
P	E	P	P	E	R	M	I	N	T		A	N	T	S
E	N	E		S	O	M	E		B	O	C	C	I	E
R	A	S	C	A	L	S		P	E	R	K			
		O	W	L		F	I	L	B	E	R	T	S	
C	O	L	T	S		C	U	L	L		R	O	O	T
O	B	I	T		M	A	D	L	Y		J	O	K	E
B	O	Z	O		O	R	G	S		K	A	S	E	M
B	E	A	N	P	O	L	E		B	I	C			
	C	A	S	S		M	U	S	K	R	A	T		
A	R	C	A	D	E		E	R	R	S		A	L	A
L	O	O	N		J	A	W	B	R	E	A	K	E	R
S	O	L	D		A	L	A	I		R	H	E	T	T
O	K	A	Y		W	I	N	G		S	A	R	A	S

43

S	L	A	M		S	E	R	B		S	W	A	L	E
L	A	D	E		O	D	O	R		T	I	G	E	R
O	V	E	N		N	I	N	A		A	S	H	E	S
P	A	N	A	M	A	C	A	N	A	L	P	A	R	T
		T	A	R	T		D	D	A	Y				
R	E	L	A	Y	S		S	N	A	G		A	P	E
E	X	U	R	B		S	W	A	G		A	L	A	S
S	U	M	M	E	R	T	I	M	E	P	L	A	Y	S
O	D	E	S		A	O	N	E		E	M	C	E	E
D	E	N		S	I	N	G		A	W	A	K	E	N
			A	P	S	E		A	M	E	N			
P	R	O	C	E	E	D	S	P	E	E	D	I	L	Y
A	O	R	T	A		E	A	R	N		I	D	E	A
U	L	C	E	R		A	R	I	D		N	O	E	L
L	E	A	D	S		F	I	L	S		E	L	S	E

44

C	R	O	C		C	I	R	C	A		S	L	O	T
H	O	U	R		E	N	A	C	T		W	E	A	R
O	U	T	T	O	L	U	N	C	H		A	N	T	I
R	E	D	S	H	I	R	T		L	A	N	D	H	O
D	S	O		A	C	E		P	E	R	K			
		B	R	A	D	P	I	T	T		A	G	E	
O	P	E	R	A		L	E	I		C	L	I	P	
M	A	D	A	S	A	M	A	R	C	H	H	A	R	E
A	L	A	N		V	A	T		A	I	S	L	E	
N	O	M		B	I	G	A	M	I	S	T			
			A	L	A	I		A	N	S		S	D	I
A	L	C	O	T	T		I	N	C	L	I	N	E	D
N	E	A	R		O	F	F	T	H	E	W	A	L	L
K	A	N	T		R	I	F	L	E		A	C	H	E
A	R	E	A		S	T	Y	E	S		S	K	I	D

162

45

```
R E T R O   A C M E   A C T S
O M A H A   M A R X   S H O O
U P P E R L I M I T   S E R B
S T E T   A G E   M I A M I
T Y R O   G O L F E R S P E G
    R N S     L A S T S
J O L I E   B R A S   H E N
E L E C T R I C I T Y W O E S
T E T   O R A L   D I T K A
    H O I S T   E S L
W H A C K S H A R D   D A L I
H A R T E   N E D   B O A T
O L G A   C A G E Y S O R T S
O V I D   O I L S   P A T I O
P E C S   G L E E   F R A N K
```

46

```
I M P S   L A T H S   R A P T
S O L O   A P I A N   O L L A
M O U N T T H E S O A P B O X
S R S   A V I D   W R E S T
      R I D   A S I S
S T R A T A   C R U D   K A Y
A R E N A   G O B I   T A R A
G E T I N T O H O T W A T E R
E A R L   R O A R   I L I A D
S T Y   B E E N   A C C E S S
      F R A Y   A R K
S T O O D   A C N E   S K I
T H R O W I N T H E T O W E L
W O O L   N O T E S   R A N K
O D D S   G R A S S   E N O S
```

47

```
L A P S E   A C I D   M E S H
U N I O N   B O R E   A C H E
C O L D T A B L E T   T R E E
I L L   R I O T   A C T U A L
D E S S E R T   L I A R
    P A Y   P O N D E R E D
F A C E T   T R U E   S O D A
O R A L   G O O S E   S A N S
W I L L   E N V Y   O P R A H
L A M B A S T E   O V A
    I N T O   P R E D I C T
R W A N D A   S E E R   S R O
A R I D   L I N C O L N L O G
M A D E   T O O K   A R E N A
S P A R   S U B S   P A T E S
```

48

```
D O R I S   A B B E   S P A M
O V U L E   L E A P   C U B A
V E H I C L E E L E V A T O R
E R R A T A   Z E A L O U S
      S Y R I A   T E N T H
D O R A   I N C H
I N U N D A T E   O U T R A N
C U S T O M E R I N V O I C E
E S T E E M   T R E A T E R S
      O L I O   O L E S
R E P E L   L A N C E
E X O T I C A   B L U R B S
F I S H E R M A N S F L O A T
E L S E   E A S E   I N D I A
R E E L   E S S O   N A S T Y
```

163

49

```
T R O T . S C A L P . A S T A
H E R R . T A B O O . S N A G
A N T I . O R O N O . C O P E
W E E P I N G W I L L O W . .
E G G . N E O . . A T E S T .
D E A L T . S L I T . D O N .
. . O R A T I O N . J I L T .
. W H O O P I N G C R A N E .
B O O M . S L A S H E D . . .
A R M . D E L I . H E I S T .
A D E L E . A A A . S P A . .
. . B A B B L I N G B R O O K
X R A Y . L O S E R . O B O E
E A S E . O P I N E . B A L I
D E E R . B E T T E . E R S T
```

50

```
R E P . W O N . D O G S H O W
O N E T I M E . E P I C U R E
O C E A N I A . S A V A G E D
M O V I E T R A I L E R . . .
E R E . S E E . . A L M S . .
R E S E T . D R E A M B O A T
. . . L O W . O A H U . G N U
A L L S T A R . R E S P O N D
B O O . A D A Y . M I S . . .
B U B B L E J E T . C I L I A
E P E E . . T E A . . O T T .
. . B A T T I N G C O A C H .
B E G O N I A . S H E A T H E
A D A P T E R . E A R T H E N
S U B S I S T . S S T . E S S
```

51

```
P A U L . A G A R . S A L A D
R A N I . N A N O . E L I S E
I R I S . D R N O . R E M I T
G E T T H E B E T T E R O F .
. . S E A L . . A N T . . . .
A M P . A N E M O N E . E V E
R O O S T . E R G . O M I T .
M O P T H E F L O O R W I T H
E S P Y . A D O . A L L A Y .
D E Y . B R A N D E D . E L L
. . S I T . E L I A . . . . .
. P U T T H E K I B O S H O N
M E R I T . T A C O . P I P E
E A G L E . C L E W . I V E S
G R E E R . H E R S . C E N T
```

52

```
B L A B . H E L E N A . W A D
L O K I . A M O R A L . O L E
O V I S . S C R I P T . R U N
C E N T I P E D E . R U M M Y
. . . R O S E S . B U R L . .
M A S O N . . C L I N I C S .
U S P S . T H R O E S . Z O E
S K I . T H E O R E M . A B A
T E D . O R A T E D . P R O M
S W E A T E R . M A D L Y . .
. R I T E . S A F E S . . . .
L U C R E . T A R A N T U L A
E R R . R E A D E R . E L A N
A D A . E R M I N E . U N I T
N U B . R E S E T S . R A N I
```

53

```
M E S A . S W A N S . T A C T
O X E N . T E N E T . A L A I
P A L A C E E N T O U R A G E
E L M . L E D A . C L O N E S
S T A T E L Y . S K A T . . .
. . A R S . C L A N . A M I
A B A C I . M E A D . I R O N
J U D I C I A L S E S S I O N
A R A T . M Y T H . T S A R S
R P M . S P A S . L E U . .
. . M E A N . L O R E L E I
I D I O M S . S O L E . O E D
T E N N I S E N C L O S U R E
E L I E . E V O K E . A S I A
M I T T . S E W E D . D Y E S
```

54

```
B O A R . P A R T . A F O O T
A B L E . A T O P . N O V A S
W O O D S T O C K . G R A T A
L E T . P O L K . T E E T E R
. . B A I L . P U R S E R S
C L O U D S . W O R S T . .
L A P S E . C R I B . H E M P
U T A H . S A Y S O . I G O R
B E L L . P U L E . B L I N I
. . E A R L Y . B A L S A M
H O M A G E S . B A S S . .
A P O G E E . L O N E . A P E
R E R U N . J U N G L E J I M
T R E E D . O R E L . B A L I
S A L S A . G E R E . B R E R
```

55

```
H A D J . H A B I T . R E A P
E Q U I . A C O R N . O R C A
M U T T . G H O S T S T O R Y
P A C T . G E M . O A S E S
. . H E L L . S C E N T . .
E N T R I E S . A L G E B R A
M O R S E . T Y R O . D R I P
O D E . S C R E E N S . O P T
T E A R . O A T S . F O U L
E S T U A R Y . S C R I M P Y
. . B R A S H . H I E S . .
S T O I C . A M I . S T A B
W I T C H H A Z E L . T I N E
A L T O . I D E A L . A C T S
N E O N . P A S T Y . S K I S
```

56

```
O N E . P M . C A R L A . A H S
D O R I A . O R E O S . R A W
E S S E X . F A C T S . E R E
S H A D E O F B L U E . A B E
S E T . D I E . I S T . C O T
A D Z . O L E A N . S N O R E
. . L U C . S E N . A D E N
C U R T A I N R A I S E R . .
O H N O . N N E . U N A . .
P L A N O . S W I S H . S S I
T O W . N A T . N E A . T A N
I R A . B L I N D A L . L E Y S
M I R . A D L A I . E E R I E
A N E . S A L V E . R A N D R
L E S . E S S E S . S H O O T
```

57

```
A M T S   A L O T   W H I G S
W A I T   P I N E   H A D E S
O G L E   P A L L   I R O N S
L I T T L E B Y L I T T L E
      S E A L   G E E
O P S   A L E R T L Y   M A D
F E T E S   O O O   M E M O
F R O M T H E G R O U N D U P
E C R U   E S E   L O O S E
R Y E   T A P R O O T   C E Y
      J A R   R A R E
  O N E S T E P A T A T I M E
A M I S S   L U T E   H O U R
S E N S E   A M O R   E T T A
K N E E L   M A R S   R A T S
```

58

```
F A C T S   E D A M   A V I D
A G L E T   N E V E   D I M E
T E A P A R T I E S   A R P A
      P E T E R F R A M P T O N
B I T E   F E Y   U T U R N
A I R   F I E   O T T   E T A
H I A T A L   A H E A D
    P A U L T S O N G A S
      U V E A S   T E M P L E
D O H   I D O   D A N   A I L
A R A B S   A R C   I C B M
M A R Y M A G D A L E N E
S C A T   I N O P E R A B L E
E L S E   D A R E   I N A I R
L E S S   E W E S   N E R D S
```

59

```
B O C A   E D E N   R H O D A
E F O R   N A T O   A U R A S
A F R U S T R A T E D M A T H
T I N   I R K S   M I S L A Y
I C E   G E E   V I A
T E A C H E R W I L L F E E L
    H T S   A N Y   A G R A
M A T E S   A L E   O T O E S
A N E W   A W L   I V S
O N L Y A F R A C T I O N O F
    S L Y   H E S   U T A
A N O P I A   T A R A   B O W
J O B S A T I S F A C T I O N
A P I A N   R A F T   E L L E
R E S T S   E R S E   N E E D
```

60

```
B A S I N   A M A H   S P A R
A P A C E   V A R Y   P U L E
S I N E W   I N F A V O R O F
E S T   S H O E   C I T R U S
S H O T G U N   E I N
      R I N   U N N E R V E D
A R O A R   G N A T   A I D A
M I D D L E O F T H E R O A D
O P I E   U L E E   S E L M A
R E N D E R E D   S O L
      M O M   K A T Y D I D
T O S S U P   S I T E   I R A
O P P O S E D T O   R I V E T
R E E L   A N E W   I N A N E
O N C E   N A N A   C A N E S
```

61

D	E	A	L	T		S	E	G	A		T	O	W	S
A	T	R	I	A		E	M	I	T		I	R	A	E
R	U	B	I	K	S	C	U	B	E		M	E	I	R
E	D	O		E	A	T		B	I	T	E	O	F	F
S	E	R	M	O	N		Z	O	N	E	S			
		E	N	J	O	I	N		T	S	A	R	S	
B	R	A	N		O	W	N		S	E	Q	U	E	L
L	I	N	T		S	E	G	N	O		U	N	D	O
O	C	T	A	V	E		E	A	R		A	T	O	P
C	H	I	L	I		P	R	Y	B	A	R			
			B	E	A	L	S		A	M	E	N	D	S
A	R	A	L	S	E	A		P	T	A		U	R	I
P	E	S	O		S	Q	U	E	E	Z	E	B	O	X
E	P	I	C		O	U	S	T		E	L	I	O	T
S	O	A	K		P	E	A	S		S	O	A	P	Y

62

S	A	M	I		A	C	T	S		O	N	S	E	T
A	D	E	N		N	O	S	Y		T	A	H	O	E
T	U	R	F		E	D	A	M		H	Y	E	N	A
E	L	G	I	N	M	A	R	B	L	E	S			
S	T	E	R	E	O		O	I	L		S	O	U	
			M	E	N	T	A	L	B	L	O	C	K	S
M	A	S		D	E	A	N			O	P	R	A	H
A	L	T	O		S	I	G	H	T		T	A	P	E
L	A	R	V	A		E	A	R	L		M	I	R	
T	R	I	A	L	B	A	L	L	O	O	N			
A	M	P		G	A	R		U	S	U	R	P	S	
		F	I	R	E	M	E	N	S	B	A	L	L	
R	I	F	L	E		N	A	R	C		I	D	E	A
A	R	D	O	R		A	M	I	E		L	O	A	M
H	E	A	P	S		S	A	C	S		E	N	D	S

63

A	S	P	S		C	H	I	C		A	L	A	M	O
D	A	L	Y		H	A	S	H		L	I	B	E	L
U	L	A	N		O	L	L	A		L	O	U	S	E
L	O	S	E	F	I	V	E	P	O	U	N	D	S	
T	O	M		O	R	E		E	R	R		H	A	L
S	N	A	R	L		S	T	A	K	E		A	G	O
			I	I	I		H	U	N		A	B	E	D
G	E	T	S	O	M	E	E	X	E	R	C	I	S	E
L	U	R	E		P	A	R			Y	E	N		
	B	A	R	E	R			C	E	A	S	E		
T	A	M		A	L	P		A	P	T		S	I	N
S	M	O	K	E	L	E	S	S	O	F	T	E	N	
S	I	E	V	E		U	R	S	A		R	U	N	E
E	A	S	E	R		G	I	L	L		E	T	N	A
E	N	T	R	Y		S	E	E	M		D	E	A	D

64

S	T	E		P	A	N	A	M	A		L	O	M	B
C	A	S		F	L	O	R	I	D		I	D	O	L
H	I	T		C	O	L	D	C	O	M	F	O	R	T
I	C	E	S		T	O	U	R		B	E	M	A	
S	H	E	O	L		O	O	N	A		E	L	F	
M	I	S	F	O	R	T	U	N	E		S	T	I	R
			T	R	I	E	S		T	W	E	E	Z	E
R	E	C	E	I	P	T		S	P	A	R	R	E	D
A	L	O	N	S	O		P	E	A	R	L			
M	E	N	S		F	O	R	T	Y	N	I	N	E	R
P	C	S		A	F	R	O			S	N	O	R	E
		T	O	O	N		N	O	T	I		G	O	A	T
H	O	L	D	T	H	E	F	O	R	T		D	S	T
E	R	E	I		O	R	E	G	O	N		L	E	O
E	S	S	E		T	Y	R	A	N	T		E	R	N

65

A	B	E	T		E	L	H	I		T	W	I	C	E
N	A	M	E		N	E	A	R		P	E	D	A	L
T	I	M	E	I	S	W	H	A	T	K	E	E	P	S
S	L	Y		G	U	I	A	N	A		V	A	S	E
		D	O	R	S			R	B	I				
A	D	M	I	R	E		E	T	I	O	L	O	G	Y
W	E	I	R		O	N	O	F	F		T	O	E	
A	L	L	T	H	E	S	T	U	F	F	F	R	O	M
R	H	O		O	I	L	E	R		L	O	S	E	
D	I	S	C	O	L	O	R		C	H	O	S	E	N
		O	D	E		G	L	U	E					
P	R	A	M		E	D	G	I	E	R		S	U	B
H	A	P	P	E	N	I	N	G	A	T	O	N	C	E
E	S	S	E	S		N	A	U	T		V	A	L	E
W	H	E	L	P		O	W	E	S		A	G	A	R

66

G	O	E	S		B	O	Z	O	S		A	L	M	S
A	N	N	A		R	O	A	C	H		B	I	A	S
R	E	D	S	N	A	P	P	E	R		A	N	T	S
O	R	I	S	O	N			L	E	A	D	E	R	
T	O	N	E	R		S	C	O	W	L		A	O	K
T	U	G	S		T	H	A	T		M	A	G	N	A
E	S	S		T	R	O	T		F	O	R	E	S	T
			W	H	I	T	E	W	I	N	E			
B	O	O	H	O	O		R	O	A	D		P	I	G
E	P	S	O	M		P	E	R	T		C	H	O	O
D	A	M		A	C	O	R	N		D	I	A	N	A
		C	O	N	S	U	L		S	U	N	S	E	T
R	I	S	E		B	L	U	E	C	H	E	E	S	E
O	T	I	S		A	O	R	T	A		M	I	C	E
M	Y	S	T		N	I	N	E	R		A	N	O	S

67

R	A	M	S		S	W	I	S	S		E	F	F	S
A	F	E	W		P	A	S	H	A		C	O	R	P
P	A	R	A	N	O	R	M	A	L		O	R	A	L
T	R	E	M	O	R			P	A	A	N	D	M	A
S	T	A	V	E			R	O	S	E	Y			
A	T	E	E			B	A	S	S	I				
P	A	L	L	M	A	L	L		T	O	T	A	L	S
P	R	E	M	I	S	E		R	U	S	H	D	I	E
S	A	V	O	R	S		P	A	N	O	R	A	M	A
			I	N	C	O	G			U	M	P	S	
S	E	P	T	A		Y	I	E	L	D				
P	A	L	O	M	A	R		A	N	K	A	R	A	
I	R	A	Q		P	A	N	A	M	A	N	I	A	N
E	T	T	U		E	N	A	T	E		O	R	Z	O
S	H	O	E		D	O	P	E	S		W	E	E	D

68

M	O	O	S		E	N	D	S		P	U	T	O	N
I	S	L	E		M	I	R	E		S	M	O	K	E
F	L	I	T		P	L	A	T		A	P	E	R	S
F	O	O	T	T	H	E	B	I	L	L		T	A	T
			L	E	A	D		N	O	T	C	H		
F	I	N	E	S	S	E	D		B	E	R	E	F	T
O	D	O		T	E	L	E	X		R	U	L	E	R
R	I	S	E		S	T	A	Y	S		Z	I	T	I
T	O	E	R	R		A	T	L	A	S		N	E	E
S	T	A	G	E	D		H	O	P	E	L	E	S	S
			R	O	V	E	R		P	L	E	A		
L	E	O		E	Y	E	T	H	I	N	G		S	U	P
A	R	U	B	A		T	O	O	N		G	O	N	E
V	I	N	Y	L		R	I	N	G		E	D	I	T
A	N	D	E	S		O	L	E	S		D	A	T	E

69

```
C A C H E . R E G I S . G A S
A C H E S . E N A C T . R U T
D R A F T D O D G E R . E G O
S E T T E E . S A B O T E U R
. . . R A H . O H E N R Y . .
H A M S . L A T E X E S . . .
E R I E . I S I N . I T S A .
W I N D I N S T R U M E N T S
. D E A N . L A I N . R I T A
. . T E R E N C E . S P U D .
S E C E D E . . H A Y . . . .
P E R S I A N S . S E A B E E
I R E . B R E E Z E A L O N G
T I E . L E A V E . R E D I G
E E K . E R R E D . S E E D Y
```

70

```
D I N A H . A S I A . P S I S
E C O L I . F O N D . A H M E
L E V A R . A R C H . T O R T
I R O N S I N T H E F I R E .
. . . A U T O . R E N T . . .
. S A L T O F T H E E A R T H
S P I D E R . R U S T . A R E
H O R A . J A M . P N I N . .
O R C . D I E S . S W A G E S
D E A D I N T H E W A T E R .
. . . V E E P . N A S T . . .
. C A S T L E I N T H E A I R
E L L A . A C N E . O R A T E
L O R D . C O R A . U N B A G
S T Y E . E N I D . T S A R S
```

71

```
A B E L . C A M P S . O A T S
D I E U . O R A L E . G N A T
D A R T . R I C E R . E D G Y
I F I H A D A H A M M E R . .
C R E E L . O D O R . E B B .
T A R R I E S . S N I F T E R
. . B O E R . E T R E . . . .
B L O W I N I N T H E W I N D
. . . L O V E . S E A T . . .
A B E T T E D . A T H E I S T
H E R . A L A S . E L M E R .
. P E T E R P A U L M A R Y .
B E A M . C R A G S . O R E S
T R I M . T E R R E . R E N T
L A D Y . S N E A D . E T E S
```

72

```
O S A Y . P E C S . F L A M E
C A M E . A R U M . R O L E X
H Y P O C R I T E . O P I N E
. S U M O . K E A N U . M A R
O W L E T . R E F L E C T . .
T H E N E R V E . D R O N E S
S O S . M O N A . O A T S . .
. . C O N U N D R U M . . . .
S T A B . S U E T . D D T . .
S P A R S E . I N E S C R O W
A I R L E S S . A L A M O . .
G E T . S P A T S . M I C A .
G L A S S . M A N N E Q U I N
E E R I E . B R I O . U L N A
D R E D D . A S P S . E A S T
```

169

73

HAIKU · VERB · ABBA
OBOES · AGAR · PLAN
YOUPUTSOMETHING
IRAS · DOINGS
HIS · PLATO · ODIST
INTHECLOSET
CARED · OLE · POSH
KNEW · COLOR · EXPO
SEWN · AOK · COILS
AWHILEANDIT
HOKUM · STERN · ETS
ATONES · EGAD
SHRINKSTWOSIZES
TEAT · IOWA · TBARS
ERNE · PLOY · ASPEN

74

CABOB · ANEW · MIME
OHARA · SERA · IDOL
LOREN · ZHART · CEOS
DYE · JEEP · ETHANE
CODS · AREA
BATHES · COLLEGES
ARRAS · FARO · LUCE
SEER · PESTO · JILT
ETAL · ETTA · BFLAT
DETENTES · GROTTO
SEED · PAIX
DEALER · BARD · IDO
OLGA · SHERYLCROW
FARM · OINK · ERODE
FLAB · NETS · SYNOD

75

RAID · ABATE · VIES
OSLO · BRIAN · ACTI
CHILLBUMPS · LEAR
SEALIONS · EDIBLE
ITTO · SMEAR
RICERS · CABINETS
AROSE · PILL · TARO
GEL · SCATTER · KIR
ENDS · ACES · ADEPT
DETOURED · STORES
UNSER · HAIL
BARNES · CABOOSES
ELKE · FROZENROPE
ABET · OUTER · EDIE
RAYS · REEDS · SACK